KU-532-716

APPROACHES TO PLANNING

APPROACHES TO PLANNING

Introducing Current Planning Theories, Concepts, and Issues

Ernest R. Alexander

Department of Urban Planning
The University of Wisconsin-Milwaukee

GORDON AND BREACH SCIENCE PUBLISHERS
New York • London • Paris • Montreux • Tokyo

© 1986 by Gordon and Breach Science Publishers S.A., P.O. Box 161, 1820 Montreux 2, Switzerland. All rights reserved.

Gordon and Breach Science Publishers

P.O. Box 786
Cooper Station
New York, NY 10276
United States of America

P.O. Box 197
London WC2E 9PX
England

58, rue Lhomond
75005 Paris
France

14-9 Okubo 3-chome,
Shinjuku-ku,
Tokyo 160
Japan

LEEDS POLYTECHNIC

700002996

BTP ✓

94276

17·12·87

711·01

Library of Congress Cataloging-in-Publication Data

Alexander, Ernest R.
  Approaches to planning.

  Bibliography: p.
  Includes index.
  1. Planning. I. Title.
HD87.5.A425 1986   658.4'012   86-3113
ISBN 2-88124-140-9.

ISBN 2-88124-140-9. No part of this book may be reproduced or utilized in any form or by any means, electronic or mechanical, including photocopying and recording, or by any information storage or retrieval system, without permission in writing from the publishers. Printed in the United States of America.

CONTENTS

PREFACE

This is a book on planning. Here, comprehensive planning is subsumed under a more encompassing view of planning, a view that sees planning as a generic type of human and societal activity. In this sense, the discussion of planning that follows is equally valid for the planning-related aspects of management and administration, and for both comprehensive and sectoral planning.

What this book does is present some of the thinking about planning and issues relevant to planning that have emerged in recent years. The review presented here cannot claim to be exhaustive, and will unavoidably be to some degree arbitrary and subjective, since there is as yet no agreed upon benchmark for deciding on what to include and what to leave out. Consequently, there may be ideas that could be considered valuable, or findings that someone could decide are important, that have not been included. This is because it is impossible to be all-encompassing of a field that is at the same time unbounded and constantly changing. Or it may be because, while valuable, they are not critical, in my judgment, for the picture of planning-related thought presented here, which has to be limited, of course, by constraints of space and the reader's attention.

The book also offers a conceptual format of questions that provide a framework for the material presented. With this framework I have attempted to make it easier for the reader to make some sense of the eclectic repertoire of ideas that have been generated by scholars, researchers, and practitioners over the past two decades and which make up the body of thought relating to planning today.

The reader of this book may be a student: an undergraduate for whom this selection of thoughts about planning can be an introductory overview, or a graduate student in a professional program where this review can serve as a skeleton text around which to present supplementary reading. However, I have not written this book simply as a text, but rather to share with a body of intelligent readers the thoughts on planning that have accumulated in recent years. These thoughts may also be of interest to others besides students: to scholars in other substantive aspects of planning, decision making, management, or administration, and to practitioners who may want to refresh their thinking about what it is they are doing by exposing themselves to some ideas on planning that have gained currency since they entered their professions.

Many share with me any credit due for this book, and first among them are the thinkers, scholars, researchers and practitioners who are cited, and who have contributed—and often still are contributing—to this body of planning-related thought. Second among them are my own teachers who also number among the first, but who stimulated my interest in the questions: What is planning? How is it carried out? How are plans implemented, and how can planning become more effective? Some of them do not consider themselves planners—though I count them among my colleagues— and some may well disagree with many of my characterizations of planning, planning roles, and planning contexts that follow. Their contribution may not be as evident as if I were their clone, but it has persisted nevertheless, even though our interaction was, in some cases, over ten years ago. One is John W. Dyckman, planning theorist par excellence, in whose footsteps I follow in attempting this review, but who was more modest than I am (in not completing his synthesis) though assuredly far better qualified for the task. Another is Aaron Wildavsky, who keeps the feet of planners and others rooted in reality. The third is Robert P. Biller, who sensitized me and many others to the interaction between planning and organizations. None of these, of course, should share the burden of this particular aggregation of ideas: that is my responsibility alone. Without them, however, this review would certainly have not taken the form that it did.

Finally, the encouragement of my wife and family, and the support of my colleagues in the School of Architecture & Urban Planning of the University of Wisconsin-Milwaukee, are gratefully acknowledged. Developing the planning theory course in the planning program here, teaching it and amending it in interaction with several generations of students provided an invaluable stimulus for examining others' thinking about planning, while Tony Catanese provided the first impetus for "putting it all together" in book form. All these made the task easier, as did the devoted secretarial help of Paula Hepburn and Roe Campo, and I hope that all involved will, in the outcome, find their contributions have been worthwhile.

CHAPTER 1

Introduction

Before city planning can function in a democracy, it must hurdle at least four obstacles:
a) win the approval of the public to its proposal;
b) be sufficiently influential to obtain the authorizing legislation;
c) gain cooperation as to policy, plan and detail of the necessary officials or official agencies, and
d) survive the scrutiny of the courts as to the reasonableness of the plan in its effect on property rights.
These tests will demand more than the simple technical skill of the average city planner.[1]

Since 1946, when Charles Abrams wrote this, planning has grown more rather than less complex, and the challenges to planners have multiplied. Those of us who are planners or would-be planners, if we want to see our plans implemented, cannot limit ourselves to routine technical skills. We need to know ourselves, our tasks, our context, and our environment.

When one is doing "comprehensive planning," what is actually taking place? A simple answer might be: "I'm preparing a land-use inventory, from which we'll later develop an amended zoning ordinance," or, "This population projection on which I'm working is needed for the development policy recommendations the mayor requested." Such simple answers, however, are as partial and misleading as those of the worker on

1

the cathedral who, when asked what he was doing, said: 'I'm laying bricks."

To function as effective practitioners demands an intelligent appreciation of what planning is in general, and of comprehensive planning in particular. We need to understand the planning process, and the diverse roles in it of planners, their clients—governments, organizations, and institutions, and their members: elected and appointed officials, administrators, and other experts—and the public at large and its components: community elites and workers, suburbanites and central-city poor, organized interest groups and the "silent majority," "averages," and "minorities": women, blacks and other ethnic groups, handicapped, and elderly, and the young. Finally, we need to know ourselves: Who are planners? What do they do and why do they do it? Why are they needed and allowed to do what they do?

Most of these questions do not have clear, unambiguous answers, and none of the responses is a simple, useful routine procedure, skill, or algorithm (a tool that can be directly applied to solving a particular problem). These issues are the domain of theory, and what use, you may ask, is that? I will address that question next, and then present some of the answers that have evolved in planning theory to the issues raised above.

Why Theory?—The Case for Planning Theory

"Nothing is as practical as theory" said physicist J. Robert Oppenheimer, one of the developers of the atom bomb. This statement seems paradoxical, but it begins to make sense when we appreciate what theory actually is. Theory is a way of understanding the world, a framework to organize facts and experience and interpret them in a systematic way:

> Science is built of facts the way a house is built of bricks; but an accumulation of facts is no more science than a pile of bricks is a house.[2]

Theory, then, is the blueprint we use to assemble the bricks of fact and experience into the coherent structure of understanding. But theory is not only a basis for understanding the world around us, it is also the foundation for developing skills and tools needed for application. Theory, therefore, is as essential to the practitioner as it is to the scientist.

The practitioner's application of theory in practice is the ultimate test of its validity and its value; as Mao Tse-Tung said:

> If we have a correct theory, but merely prate about it, pigeonhole it
> and do not put it into practice, then that theory, however, good, has
> no significance.[3]

This suggests one of the dimensions of the interaction between planning
and the social sciences, from which planning has obtained many of its
theories and methods. The theories developed by economists, sociologists,
urban anthropologists, social psychologists, and the like, are all valuable
contributions to our understanding of the subjects and contexts of our
planning efforts. But planning, in turn, can provide the practical arena for
confirming or refuting theory.[4]

Praxis: Theory and Practice

Practice, in turn, should be informed by theory. Practice needs theory not
only to structure the world and the environment, which are the objects
of actions, but also to explain their actions to the actors themselves. This
kind of action has been called *praxis*, from the Greek word for practice,
which as used by Aristotle, later came to denote a certain kind of practice.

Praxis in the Aristotelian sense applied to disciplines and activities
demanding more than the simple technical skill needed for producing arte-
facts—activities affecting peoples' social and political lives and their
broader environment:

> The end . . . of the practical disciplines or *praxis* is not theoretical
> knowledge. . .[it] is to change our forms of activity and bring them
> into closer approximation to the full ideal of free human activity.[5]

Planning, of course, is a discipline that this definition of praxis fits like a
glove.

In its elaboration by later thinkers the idea of praxis remained clearly
distinguished from practice as simple instrumental action, but rather saw
action as interdependent with its actors and its living context: "this praxis
always moves within a reality which reason has imagined for itself".[6]
Praxis, then, is the critical self-reflective activity of the practitioner who
recognizes that the external world, including his own tasks, values, and
norms, is the product of a stream of previous human interactions. For
such a praxis, a planner must have the understanding of planning and the
planning process that planning theory begins to provide.

Ideology and Evaluation: Theory and Action

The relationship between theory and action that is expressed in the concept of praxis is especially important for planning, as it is for other applied disciplines and professions such as engineering, education, law, and medicine. This is because planning (and these other professions) unlike the sciences, is ultimately a prescriptive, not a descriptive, activity. The planner does not aim to describe or to explain the world as it is, but rather to propose ways in which to change things in desired directions.[7]

Theory provides scientific explanations and descriptions of fact with a standard to judge whether they are true or false. For normative activities, like planning, theory is also necessary for evaluation. Both planners and their clients or consumers need a framework for judging the success or failure of planning efforts.[8] This is not as simple as it may seem, and intuitive assessments may easily be biased or plain wrong.[9]

The evaluation of planning demands a standard of reference, an explanation, or model of the planning process and its subjects, participants, and context. In short, evaluation needs the underpinning of theory.[10] Indeed, the very existence of planning as a systematic activity requires a rationale and a social legitimation: It "must be justified as the institutionalized application of rational decision-making to social affairs".[11]

Finally, because planning and planners' activities, if they have any impact at all, affect society and involve human values, planning theory cannot ignore ideology. Evaluation of success or failure, where actions change the lives of people, must relate to some perception—their own, their leaders' or representatives', the planners', or that of some "neutral" analyst, academic, or philosopher—of their needs, desires, and values. Consequently, as John Dyckman said, "the theory of planning must include some theory of the society in which planning is institutionalized".[12]

Sources of Planning Theory

There is no single agreed upon definition of planning theory, nor is there any consensus on what it includes. Just as the planning profession grew to its present configuration, drawing its members from different backgrounds, so planning theory developed by an eclectic accretion of concepts from a wide range of disciplines. Today planning theory reflects the sequence of dominant images that have succeeded one another since planning became a distinct area of endeavor.[13]

The first planners came from the ranks of the other "design professions": architecture, landscape design, and civil engineering. One concept they brought with them was utopianism: the idea that you can "design" an ideal end state, and use it to change the world to conform more closely to the utopian ideal.[14]

This utopian perspective characterized some of the early giants who influenced both the ideology of city planning and the actual forms taken by planned cities and communities: Ebenezer Howard, Frank Lloyd Wright, Le Corbusier, Lewis Mumford, and Clarence Stein.[15]

Some have suggested that this, in fact, is the most important contribution that planning can make: normative planning—presenting possible futures that articulate ultimate social and human values—as a benchmark for current policy goals.[16] Others, in turn, see the rigid, formalized plans and complex system models that are recent expressions of the utopian tradition as unresponsive to reality and handicapping society's ability to respond to uncertainty and change.[17]

Another concept was comprehensiveness, based on the realization of the interdependence of the parts that make up the whole. The architect's designs for a building had to take into account human circulation and functions, construction technology, environmental control systems such as heating and ventilation, the outside environment—climate, site geology, access and streets, other buildings—aesthetics, and symbolic communication—the Capitol's dome, the pillars of the courthouse or stock exchange, the gabled home.

Accordingly, the architect-planners were predisposed to recognize that cities were more than avenues or plazas alone, or sewers alone, or just the smell of the horse-drawn buses. They—together with their landscape designer and civil engineer colleagues—realized that a comprehensive view, which could put all the relevant separate sectoral perspectives together, was necessary. The concept of comprehensiveness runs like a scarlet thread through the web of planning throughout its development and growth,[18] and it will be a central theme in this discussion.

Subsequently in the evolution of the planning profession, the social sciences made their contribution. As early as 1928 planners realized the need to "draw on the several arts and sciences, including architecture, political economy, the science of government, sanitary science, physical geography, and publicity, public movements and organizations."[19]

But the real thrust of social science inputs into planning theory and methods came later, in the 1950s and 1960s. Economics contributed ideas about equity and the public interest (from welfare economics) and ab

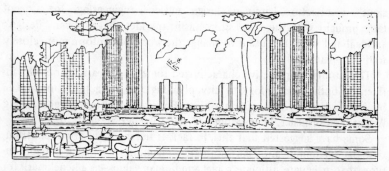

An "ideal city": The business district of Le Corbusier's "Contemporary City" as seen from one of the terraced cafes surrounding the station square (1922); from "Plan for a City of 3 Million Inhabitants", *Oevre Complete de 1910-1929*.

Source: Le Corbusier 1910-60 (Editions Girsberger, Zurich, 1960) p. 291. Copyright permission (?) La Fondation LeCorbusier, Andre Wogensky. Pres, Paris.

decision making and analysis, and the public aggregation of values (from decision and utility theory).[20] The findings of psychologists, sociologists, and political scientists about how choices are made and implemented by individuals, groups, organizations, communities, governments, and societies were also found relevant for planning. From these disciplines planning theory has adopted ideas about small group relations, organizational design and behavior, bureaucracy, community decision making, and intergovernmental relations.[21]

As this brief review shows, it is a diverse and eclectic body of knowledge that we today call "planning theory," and most of it has its roots in other disciplines. Undoubtedly, we will continue to incorporate relevant findings from these disciplines and apply them to planning, at the same time that planning scholars and practitioners are developing theory by exploring the planning process, its contexts, and its outcomes.

ng Theory: Scope and Integration

is, planning theory addresses a whole range of issues. These as follows: *definitional*—What is planning?; *substantive*— about what we are planning, and for whom we are hat do we know about how planning takes place, and how plans are implemented?; and *normative*—How do we plan, and why should we plan?

Planning theory can be seen as broad enough to include all the above, or it can be more limited. Any definition must be arbitrary to some extent, and will depend, largely, on how one views planning. A broad perspective may see planning as a generic process in itself: as a particular mode of action. On the other hand, some theorists, and many practitioners, prefer to limit their view of planning to a particular aspect, such as, for example, environmental regulation.[22] Such definitional differences, some of which will be addressed below, naturally make a good deal of difference in one's definition of theory.

The substantive aspects of planning are the hardest to delimit: They can range into areas as divergent as housing, transportation, health services, and economic development policy. Among major relevant substantive fields addressed in one planning theory text are urban growth, neighborhood units, zoning, and the physical environment.[23] Another anthology divides up the field by functional sectors: physical, social, public policy, and economic planning.[24]

Here we will not deal with the substantive aspects of planning theory. One reason is that even the most modest attempt to do so would take us much further afield than the limits of available space would permit. But I also agree with those who hold that the proper areas of concern of planning theory are the procedural and normative aspects of planning.[25]

X   The core of planning theory is the planning process: how should and do people plan? This question applies to individuals, groups, firms, and governments. A planning process is responsible for someone's deliberate career decisions, a family's household budget or vacation itinerary, a club's roster of events, a corporation's marketing strategy or production schedule, a city's capital improvement program, a state water resources plan, and national policies in energy, environment, defense, and human services.

Planning theory explores the planning process and examines its components: What are they? How do they interrelate? How are they affected by the context of planning efforts? How do they determine planning outcomes? All these affect the question of how planning should be done: planning prescriptions that are divorced from reality are utopian, and are likely to be impossible to carry out.

At the same time, in translating descriptions of planning behavior into norms for planning activities, it is important to keep the distinction clear.

The *descriptive* aspect of planning theory and its findings ("this is how it is") has to pass through an *evaluative* filter ("I think it's fine" or "I think it's terrible") to arrive at *normative* prescriptions ("this is how it ought to be") of how planning is to be done. Failure to distinguish clearly between these results in confusion in the best case, and, in the worst, wishful thinking or implicit support for the status quo.

Analysis of the planning process leads to questions about planning models and planners' roles. What characteristics in the situations where planning takes place affect planning outcomes? How can we apply our understanding of planning models, contexts, and roles to become more effective planning practitioners?

Another question addressed by planning theory is the rationale for planning: Why do we plan? This question, in turn, raises issues of ethics and values, issues that cannot be divorced from the social context in which planning takes place. When, we may ask, is it better to plan—to intervene in an ongoing process in order to affect its future state in a desired direction—and when is it better not to plan, to leave well enough alone?

The rationale for planning also raises the question of legitimacy: professional planners, after all, do not plan for themselves, but for others. What entitles them to do this, and, by implication, to make or direct social choices? Other issues also arise when we address this question.[26] Who actually plans—inquires about public and client participation in the planning process. The question, "To whom are the planners accountable for planning decisions?" has been asked, in another form, since the development of the administrative apparatus of the Roman empire: *Quis custodiet ipsos custodes*?—Who will guard the guardians?

These are the questions that will be addressed here. Though they are interrelated, the eclectic nature of planning theory has so far resisted integration. There is no "general theory of planning"; indeed, serious observers have expressed doubts whether the development of such a theory is even possible.[27] Accordingly, each issue will be taken up and explored in turn.

They will be discussed from the perspective of the practitioner of comprehensive planning, viewing comprehensive planning as a special form of planning activity. Comprehensive planning, in this view, is not limited to a particular type of planning practice, such as comprehensive physical planning or the preparation of master land-use plans. Rather, it is any type of planning that is not exclusively sectorial; that is, planning that recognizes the interdependence of multiple sectors and functions in developing strategies of action for a particular type of complex problem.

In this sense, we can talk about comprehensive land-use planning: the development of regulatory, developmental, and conservation strategies for land, taking into account the interactions between land—or, more broadly, the built and physical environment—and its inhabitants, with their demographic, economic, social, and cultural characteristics, and their institutions, norms, and values. Similarly, we can refer to comprehensive health planning, or comprehensive social or economic planning. Each of these approaches focuses on a particular functional or institutional domain, but each of them recognizes the interdependence of the parts making up the human-social-environmental and urban-regional system as a whole.

Notes

1. C. Abrams, *The Future of Housing* (New York: Harper & Bros., 1946).
2. Poincare, 1905.
3. Mao Tse-Tung, 1937.
4. R. S. Bolan, "The Practitioner as Theorist: The Phenomenology of the Professional Episode," *Journal of the American Planning Association* 46 (3), (July 1980): 261-274; pp. 261-264.
5. Aristotle, quoted in R. Bernstein, *Praxis and Action* (Philadelphia: University of Pennsylvania Press, 1971) 316.
6. J. Habermas, *Theory and Practice* (J. Viertel, trans.) (London: Heinemann, 1974), 178.
7. D. Eversley, *The Planner in Society: The Changing Role of a Profession* (London: Faber & Faber, 1973): 229-236.
8. A. B. Wildavsky, "If Planning is Everything, Maybe It's Nothing," *Policy Sciences*, 4(2) (Summer 1973) 137-153.
9. E. R. Alexander, "If Planning Isn't Everything, Maybe It's Something," *Town Planning Review*, 52(2) (April 1981): 131-142, pp. 133-134.
10. I. L. Horowitz, "Social Planning and Social Science," *Planning Theory in the 1980's: A Search for Future Directions*. (R. W. Burchell and G. Sternlieb, eds.), (New Brunswick, N.J.: Rutgers University Center for Urban and Policy Research, 1978), 53-60.
11. John W. Dyckman, "Introduction to Readings in the Theory of Planning: The State of Planning Theory in America" (mimeo draft, n.d.), 9.
12. John W. Dyckman, "The Practical Uses of Planning Theory," *Journal of the American Institute of Planners* 35 (Sepbember 1969): 300.
13. Thomas D. Galloway and Riad G. Mahayni, "Planning Theory in Retrospect: The Process of Paradigm Change," *Journal of the American Institute of Planners* 43 (January 1977); 62-71.
14. D. Reisman, "Some Observations on Community Plans and Utopia," *Individualism Reconsidered and Other Essays*, (Glencoe, Ill.: Free Press, 1954), 70-98.

15. M. Meyerson, "Utopian Traditions and the Planning of Cities," *Daedalus*, 90(1) (Winter 1961): 180-193. L. Reissman, *The Urban Process: Cities in Industrialized Societies*, (New York: Free Press, 1970) 39-68.
16. H. Ozbekhan, "The Triumph of Technology: 'Can' Implies 'Ought'," *Planning for Diversity and Choice* (S. Anderson, ed.) (Cambridge, Mass.: MIT Press, 1968).
17. R. Boguslaw, *The New Utopians*, (Englewood Cliffs, N.J.: Prentice-Hall, 1965).
18. M. Scott, *American City Planning Since 1880* (Berkeley: University of California Press, 1969) 73-75, 100, 110, 176, 227-228, 476-482, 531-536, 554 ff.
19. M. Scott (1969) pp. 265-266.
20. R. Zeckhauser and E. Schaefer, "Public Policy and Normative Economic Theory," *The Study of Policy Formation* (R. A. Bauer and K. J. Gergen, eds.), (New York: Free Press, 1968).
21. G. Gutenschwager, *Planning and Social Theory: A Selected Bibliography* (Monticello, Illl.: Council of Planning Librarians Exchange Bibliography No. 179). L. D. Mann, "Social Science Advances and Planning Applications," *Journal of the American Institute of Planners*, 28(6) (November 1972).
22. M. Hebbert, "Four Approaches to the Planning Theory Syllabus," *The Content of a Planning Theory Course: Seminar Papers* (Oxford: Oxford Polytechnic, Dept. of Town Planning, 1976).
23. M. C. Branch, *Urban Planning Theory* (Stroudsbrug, Penn.: Dowden, Hutchinson & Ross, 1975).
24. R. W. Burchell and G. Sternlieb (eds.), *Planning Theory in the 1980's: A Search for Future Directions*, (New Brunswick, N.J.: Rutgers University-Center for Urban Policy Research, 1978).
25. A. Faludi, *Planning Theory* (Oxford: Pergamon, 1973). J. W. Dyckman, "Introduction to Readings," in *The Theory of Planning*: The State of Planning Theory in America, mimeo n.d., pp. 3-6.
26. G. C. Hemmens, "New Diretions in Planning Theory," *Journal of the American Planning Association*, 46(3), (July 1980): 259-260.
27. H. Rittel and M. Webber, "Dilemmas in a General Theory of Planning," *Policy Sciences*, 4(2) (June 1973): 155-169. S. J. Mandelbaum, "A Complete General Theory of Planning is Impossible," *Policy Sciences*, 11(1) (August 1979): 59-71.

CHAPTER 2
Rationality and Decision

"Planning has always seen itself as an agent of rationality in society",[1] so before we can discuss planning, a diversion is necessary. To understand planning and the planning process, we must first know about rationality: What is it? What are its uses and limitations? How is rationality involved in individual and social decision making?

Rationality and Its Axioms

Rationality is a central feature of the planning process with which we have become familiar. We usually think of rationality as something good. To most people, being irrational means, at best, to be a bit deviant or strange, at worst, to be mad. When planning lays claim to rationality, then, it seems to be adopting popular values. But this is not really what rationality (in the sense that it relates to planning) is about.

Rather, rationality is a way of thinking about problems, a type of logic related to the concept of rationalism, which has been a central theme of Western thinking since the renaissance. Rationalism is identified with a scientific approach to analysis and with a particular way of problem solving.[2] This way of problem solving—the rational decision making model—requires people using it to consider what they ought to do in the light of what it is they want to accomplish. In other words, rationality demands the systematic consideration and evaluation of alternative means in the light of the preferred goals they are to achieve.

Seen in this way, of course, rationality is neither good nor bad. It is value-neutral, because it is not associated with any particular value, though it demands consideration of values. It is a tool, and, like any tool, whether it is good or bad depends on the uses to which it is put.

In its simplest form, rationality is a way of choosing the best means to attain a given end. This type of rationality, called "instrumental rationality," enables the choice of optimal means to achieve given goals. Often this type of problem has a determinate solution, through simple or complex algorithms like those used, for example, by engineers.

In a more comprehensive view, however, rationality includes evaluation and choice between goals as well as relating them to the individual's, organization's, or society's ultimate values. This kind of rationality has been called "substantive"[3] —or "value rationality"[4]:

> Action is instrumentally rational when the end, the means, and the secondary results are all rationally taken into account and weighed. This involves rational consideration of alternative means to the end, of the relations of the end to secondary consequences, and finally of the relative importance of different possible ends. Choice between alternative and conflicting ends may well be determined in a value rational manner.[5]

Naturally, substantive rationality is particularly important in planning, which usually involves multiple and often conflicting objectives.

The use of rationality is not intrinsically related to success or failure: There is no guarantee that choices arrived at rationally will produce the desired outcomes. In fact, many such choices would be the same if they had been arrived at intuitively.

Rational analysis is simply a tool that enables us to make choices according to certain standards of consistency and logic, and helps us to communicate the reasons for our decisions. In planning, rationality also implies that a plan, a policy, or a strategy for action is based on valid assumptions, and includes all relevant information relating to the facts, theories, and concepts on which it is based.[6]

The rational decision model is helpful in providing a systematic framework for putting together the facts and judgments that determine our choice of a course of action. Such choices are here called decisions, but it is important to remember that decisions usually involve many people in a variety of roles. The analyst or planner may apply decision analysis to arrive at a conclusion on the desired course of action under a given set of circumstances, but it is usually the executive official or decision making group in an organization or institution that adopts such recommendations and sets in motion their implementation. In making this distinction, Lichfield and his associates have called the former "decision makers," while calling the latter the "decision takers".[7]

Rational decision analysis combines the major elements that make up any decision, and is based on certain standards of logic and consistency, which simplify the complexities of situations and values. These standards are called the *axioms* of rational decision.[8]

The first axiom deals with the expression of values. Preferences must be transitive; that is, they must be ranked in order from best to worst. For example, if you prefer steak to fish, and fish to corn, and steak to corn, your preferences can be ranked: steak—fish—corn, and they are transitive. In this case you can use rational decision analysis to choose between these items on a menu, though it is unlikely that you would need to do so.

But if you happen to prefer corn to steak and steak to fish, while still liking fish better than corn, your preferences are not transitive. This does not mean you are abnormal: There are many well-documented situations where intransitive preferences prevail.[9] It only means that rational decision analysis cannot be used to make choices involving such types of preference orderings.

The next axiom states the independence of probabilities and utilities. In other words, one's assessment of the likelihood of a certain event or outcome—its probability—should be unaffected by the value assigned to that occurrence, expressing the degree to which it is preferred or dreaded—its utility. We ignore this axiom when indulging in wishful thinking, expecting unlikely outcomes because we desire them. The mirror image is the "sour grapes" syndrome: pretending to downgrade the utility of an outcome that is actually wished for, but improbable.

The irrelevance of unaffected outcomes is the third axiom. This means that outcomes or events that are not changed by one's choice of options need not be taken into consideration. This axiom seems intuitively obvious, but it is often ignored. For example, planning studies that collect data according to some predetermined format or checklist frequently omit considering the uses, if any, to which the information assembled with such effort is to be put.

Testing the possible variables proposed for study, and considering whether they are likely to affect the relevant choices, is how we apply the axiom of the irrelevance of unaffected outcomes. If the choice on a given day, for instance, is between walking to work and riding a bicycle, relevant factors may be the weather, the time available for the journey, traffic conditions, and so on. The state of the economy, though crucial for many other decisions, is irrelevant to this particular choice and may, therefore, safely be ignored. This illustration displays a simple, even trivial, decision. But this axiom is invaluable as a criterion for setting bounds to any decision analysis. Such bounds are of increasing importance in determining the information needs of decisions as problems become more complex, problems that, without such limits, would be insoluble.

The inadmissibility of dominated choices is the last axiom, without which the whole exercise of rational analysis would be pointless. This axiom dictates that, if rational analysis shows one option to be superior to all the others being evaluated, another alternative cannot be chosen. Again, this should be so intuitively obvious as to go without saying, but the rules of formal logic demand every requirement to be clearly spelled out.

With the framework of logic and consistency provided by the four axioms of rationality, we can use decision analysis to simplify problems of choice, without changing or distorting their essential relevant components. Such analysis, however, will only yield useful results if its information base incorporates sound judgments and reflects real preferences.

Decision Analysis and Rational Choice

Choices are made under any one of three different conditions, and it is up to the decision maker to recognize the situation he is in. *Certainty* covers those situations when we know our preferences, recognize the available options, and are sure about their effects. An example of choice under certainty is selecting an item from the menu in a familiar restaurant. Any uncertainty about the quality of the food or the relative taste of different dishes can be eliminated, and the only factor relevant to our decision is our preference. Though such decisions may be critical in planning a gourmet dinner with friends, they are usually too trivial to need the heavy guns of decision analysis.

More common as subjects of decision analysis are situations involving *risk*. Under conditions of risk, we know too little to be certain about events and outcomes, but we have enough information to estimate probabilities. Decision analysis provides a framework for combining these probability estimates with our preference rankings, as described below, to enable us to make a rational choice.[10]

Under uncertainty, even probabilities of events cannot be assessed. This makes such situations rare candidates for decision analysis, though some have suggested how this might be done.[11] The amount of information needed to transform a state of uncertainty into a situation of risk has been the subject of a good deal of argument. A respectable school of thought, however, holds that even estimates based on intuitive hunches and experience are usable information.[12]

In decisions made under any of these conditions, a major factor is the ranking of our preferences: these are expressed as *utilities*. Utility is the value we assign to the outcome of an action or event. It may be unquantifiable, when we can only compare an outcome qualitatively—that is, as better or worse—with the relative value of other outcomes. We can appreciate this problem, for example, when we compare notes on members of the opposite sex (though attempts at quantification crop up even here: the 1980 film *10* is a case in point).

Utility may be quantifiable, when we can estimate how much better or worse one option is than another on some abstract scale: we can call these units of measurements *utils*. Or utility can be equated with a concrete output that adequately expressed the satisfaction derived from the different possible outcomes. A generally valued common unit of exchange, such as money, fills this role in many analyses. But "money does not equal happiness" holds true here too, and the linear transformation of money into ity may conceal fallacies and lead to wrong choices.[13]

The *expected utility* of an outcome is determined by multiplying its utility by the probability of its occurrence. The likelihood of a particular outcome occurring also depends on relevant factors in the environment that affect the impact of our actions, but over which we have no control. These factors can range from quite simple to highly complex, and our decision analysis is often critically dependent on the quality of our estimates of these factors, which can be grouped as "states of nature."

A simple example will show how all these elements work in decision analysis to allow a rational choice between alternative actions. Suppose we have to choose between taking an umbrella to work (UMB) or leaving it at home (NONE). The relevant environmental factor is whether it will rain or stay clear. We will call these two alternative states of nature RAIN or DRY. The weather forecaster predicts a 70% likelihood of showers; we can therefore assign the probability of 0.7 to RAIN and 0.3 to DRY.

We also have to express our preference for each of four possible outcomes. This may be done in a variety of ways, but here we will simply assign scores in utils to symbolize the value of each outcome. The outcome UMB/RAIN means that we take an umbrella and it rains. This would give us a good deal of satisfaction, and it gets a score of 3. UMB/DRY involves the nuisance of carrying a useless umbrella to work; it is a cost, but not a heavy one, so it gets a -1. NONE/RAIN is clearly the worst outcome: a thorough soaking, valued at -5. NONE/DRY also has a positive impact, and gets a score of 3.

All these elements are combined into a matrix as shown in Table 1. We are now able to aggregate our values with our estimates of the likelihood of events, apply one or more decision criteria, and choose our preferred option. The decision criteria we use will depend on subjective factors: optimism, aversion to risk, and so on.

One criterion would be to choose the action with the largest total expected value, that is, the largest sum of expected utilities of all alternative outcomes for an option. In the example, the highest total expected utility is for UMB (1.8), so the umbrella is clearly the preferred option. Another common (and pessimistic) criterion is called the minimax. It means choosing the option with the highest minimum expected value. Which action, in other words, will yield the highest benefits if the worst case for that option should occur? For UMB, the worst is DRY (-0.3); for NONE, it is RAIN (-3.5). The higher minimum expected value is associated with UMB, so that is the action we should choose.[14]

We used two different decision criteria and each time came to the same conclusion. Our choice of an action, in other words, was not "sensitive" to our choice of a decision criterion. Given the weather report in this case, anyone with any common sense would have taken the umbrella. Most real decision problems are much more complex, however, and analysis can then be of real value in arriving at a rational choice and communicating its rationale.

Rational decision analysis is the theoretical foundation for most planning analyses. Many sophisticated methods used in planning, policy analysis, and program evaluation—such as benefit-cost analysis, cost-effectiveness analysis, investment analysis, and impact analysis[15]—are based on the components of the simple analysis illustrated above.

Of course, as problems become more complex, each factor has to be decomposed into multiple components. This often demands a great deal of data that frequently have to be processed using computers, and the pos-

Table 1 Matrix: Sample Decision Analysis

Courses of Action	RAIN (0.7)		DRY (0.3)		Total Expected Utils
	Utilities	Expected Utils	Utilities	Expected Utils	
UMB	3	2.1	−1	−0.3	1.8
NONE	−5	− 3.5	3	0.9	− 2.6

State of Nature (probability)

sibilities of error are compounded.[16] Most planning-related issues, too, are in the public domain, where assigning values to utilities, for example, becomes an exercise in collective judgment. A decision on the best type of development for a lakefront area, for example, or the choice of an appropriate solid-waste disposal site, or the selection of one among several proposed programs to reduce crime in an inner-city neighborhood, is not the kind of problem for which one individual, or an isolated analyst, can provide a solution.

While decision analysis, and the techniques that have been derived from it, can be used to enhance the level of public debate, ultimately such issues are matters of societal choice, of deciding on action to be taken by an organization, a community, or a unit of government. Here we are leaving the realm of individual decision making, and entering the domain of collective choice.

Collective Choice: A Political Process

Until now we have been discussing rational choices made by individuals or social units treated as homogeneous undifferentiated wholes. But this is not at all what social units are; even the smallest group is made up of different individuals with different traits, interests, and goals.

One person's rational choice is still a step away from the common rational choice of any societal group. The group's choice has to be made by aggregating individual preferences, and for its common decision to qualify as rational it has to meet certain conditions besides conformance to the axioms described above.

The group decision has to reflect the bias of the preferences of the individuals making up the group, and the aggregation process must be sensitive enough to respond to changes in individual preferences with corresponding changes in the group's choice. The process must also meet these requirements, whatever the distribution of individual choices. Finally, the aggregation process should be democratic; that is, the preferences of people with power or prestige cannot determine the group's choice, nor can a decision be imposed by dictatorial fiat.

Kenneth Arrow proved in his "Impossibility Theorem" that no system can be devised that completely conforms to these requirements.[17] Consequently, we have to admit that no strictly rational system can exist of aggregating individual preferences into social choices, unless some of the conditions are relaxed.[18]

In fact, as we know, social choices are made all the time, although it is difficult to determine group preferences by aggregating individual values, let alone find a fair way of doing so. In most groups the choice is strongly affected by the relative status or power of participants, and the final issue is often effectively decided by the person with the most "clout." Policy for governments or corporations is usually decided by the apparently fair process of voting, but voting systems have their anomalies, too—for example, it is possible for a U.S. President to be elected by a minority of the popular vote.

Social choices, then, are made by a political process. This process does not incorporate a logically necessary and obvious aggregation of individual or subunit preferences. In some countries, political decisions are made by a parliament or congress elected on a constituency basis (and a minority vote can obtain a majority of representatives!) while others elect their legislators by a system of proportional representation. In many organizations, institutions, and governments, incumbents of particular roles or units that control specific resources have more input into collective decisions than others with less influence.

The political process, then, is not rational in the sense presented above, or in a way that we can expect of individual decisions. Rather, it blends the values of individual and group participants through organization, commitment, and power as well as bargaining, cooperation, and conflict resolution.[19] Rationality may be deployed in analysis, in the preparation of plans and the presentation of proposals. But the political process, not rational choice, is the vehicle by which most planning proposals are adopted and implemented, a fact that planners forget at their peril.[20]

Decision Making—Ideal and Actual

Rationality involves, as we have said, deliberate selection among possible courses of action by evaluating these options in terms of the goals they are designed to achieve. The rational model, as it is usually envisaged, assumes that objectives can be identified and articulated, that the outcomes of alternative strategies can be projected and their expected utilities assessed by some goal-related objective criteria, and that the respective probability of occurrence of relevant conditions can be predicted on the basis of available information.

Of course, in different contexts this model may be applied in different ways. Conventionally, the rational model is often associated with "material" goals and quantitative analysis, and sometimes also with elaborate mathematical and microeconomic models. However, intrinsically, this does not have to be so. The developer who is figuring the potential profit of alternative investments on the back of an envelope, or the archbishop who is looking at various designs for a cathedral in terms of which will contribute to "the greater glory of God" may be making their decisions no less rationally than the officials adopting recommendations supported by their planners' benefit-cost analysis.

Rational problem solving consists of a number of stages that link ideas to action. The idea may be the perception of a problem, the articulation of objectives and goals, or the recognition of an unused resource or opportunity. Depending on how the process was stimulated, the stages may occur in various orders. Often they are also linked by feedback loops, when a prior choice has to be reconsidered in the light of new information or changed values.

These stages involve: diagnosing the problem and articulating objectives and goals; analyzing the environment and identifying relevant resources and constraints; designing alternative problem solutions, strategies, or courses of action; projecting the likely outcomes of these alternatives; and evaluating them in the light of goal-related criteria. Finally the process results in a choice that is realized through action implementing the selected alternative.[21]

Since the stages of the rational decision-making process are no different from the "classical" steps of the planning process, more detailed discussion of each stage will be deferred. But, before we unquestioningly adopt this model as the general basis for rational planning and decision making, we must ask ourselves several questions. First, *do* people actually make decisions in this way? We have already seen that, when we are dealing with collective choices, in groups, organizations, or societies, they do not. Second, even if they do not, *could* individuals, groups, or organizations make their choices using this model of the decision-making process, and would it be better if they did so? A great deal of thought and study has been devoted to these questions, and cogent objections have been raised to the rational model, both as a realistic description of human behavior, and as a feasible prescription for action.

A well-founded critique of rational problem solving has been advanced by Herbert Simon, who suggests that no real decision-making process can meet the demands of rationality: complete information and the simultaneous consideration of all possible alternatives. Accordingly, people "satisfice": that is, they discover and consider options one at a time, using as an evaluation standard a flexible "aspiration level" rather than rigid, predetermined goals.

Not only is "satisficing" how individuals and organizations actually make decisions, according to Simon, but it is also an approach that makes sense. After all, searching through an infinite set of possible alternatives, as required by the rational model, may be an endless process, and there is no guarantee that a solution will be discovered or designed that achieves the predetermined goals. On the other hand, the mutual adjustment of aspirations and possible courses of action ensures that a feasible choice will finally be made. If objectives are set too high to be met by the options that prove to be available, the aspiration level can be lowered to "fit" the best of the alternatives. Conversely, if it proves unexpectedly easy to achieve one's ends with one of a repertoire of strategies, the goals can be raised and the search continue for a superior option.[22]

Lindblom and his followers adopted a similar point of departure for attacking the rational model, which Lindblom calls the "synoptic," or "root" approach. They suggest an alternative as a more realistic description of decision making by individuals and organizations, and as a more feasible and desirable approach to complex problems. This model is called "disjointed incrementalism."

"Disjointed incrementalism" is very different from the rational model. Where the latter requires the decision maker to develop all possible alternatives—or, at least, a substantial range of options—the "incrementalist" decision maker develops only a few possible strategies, and none of them differs very radically from the status quo. The evaluation of these options then focuses on their differences from one another and from the existing state of affairs, rather than, as under the rational approach, analyzing each alternative as a whole.

The rationale for this approach is twofold. First, decision makers in reality find it impossible to deal with the mass of information the rational approach would require for problems of any complexity, so they do not even try. Second, they do not perceive as feasible courses of action that differ radically from what they are used to, or ones that lie outside the narrow range imposed by institutional constraints.[23] So, for example, addressing the problems of an economic recession in the United States by nationalizing industry is a solution too radical even to be considered, according to the "incremental" approach, though the rational model might demand its analysis as a potentially optimal solution.

One illustration of the differences between "disjointed incrementalism" and the rational approach can be found in the area of budgeting. The rational approach would prescribe what has been recently called "zero-base" budgets: costing out and comparing alternative programs in totality, with nothing taken for granted.[24] In fact, most observers have found that budget decisions are actually taken "at the margin"; that is, the alternatives that are compared by decision makers are whether to increase or decrease last year's budget by 5% or 10%. Only this simplifying mechanism enables legislators and administrators to cope with complexity and their overload of information.[25]

This reasoning is quite persuasive, and research has shown that "disjointed incrementalism" prevails in many situations.[26] But its claim to be the only realistic description of decision behavior has been disputed. Enough exceptions have been observed[27] to limit "disjointed incrementalism" to contexts that, though frequent, are not universal. Such contexts display well-defined institutions, continuity of social and organizational norms, a plural political system, and gradual change which creates problems, but ones that can be remedied by incremental solutions.[28] In fact, these contexts are rather like the American governmental and corporate bureaucracies that were the original objects of Lindblom's observation.

Though originally presented just as a description of how decisions are actually made, "disjointed incrementalism" also claimed to be a normative prescription of how choices should be made. The rationale for this was less persuasive, limited, basically, to "it is so, so it is good."[29] This was pointed out by several observers, who accused the proponents of this approach of a conservative bias, and of providing implicit support for a possibly less than ideal status quo.[30] As a result, some modifications have been proposed, like Steinbruner's "cybernetic" model, which recognizes the importance of the decision context.[31] Etzioni, also responding to the limitations of "disjointed incrementalism" suggested it is only one element in his "mixed scanning" model, which we will discuss in more detail later.

Another series of objections to the rational approach to problem solving rest on the point that neither the world, nor our behavior, are as simple as this model seems to make them. Complexity and ambiguity are everywhere, and they are increasing with the breakdown, virtually complete in modern post-industrial societies like the United States, of traditional social relationships and values:

> The police officer can no longer be sure of the viciousness of the homosexual, and the welfare agency may be urged to organize the poor to conduct rent strikes and to sue the city for nonfeasance.

The stable world of administrative commonsense is unhinged. . . and . . .has changed into one of endless relativity, grey and full of doubt.[32]

Uncertainty, too abounds. In theory, the transformation of any information on the world out there and the outcomes of alternative actions into probability estimates is possible. But in practice, outcomes may be critically affected by the reliability of these assessments.[33]

Friend and Jessop describe three types of uncertainty.[34] The first is uncertainty about the environment, which affects the possible outcomes of alternative actions. This is the kind of uncertainty that has bedevilled freeway projects based on projections of motorization rates extrapolated from the 60s, or development projects premised on population growth that fails to materialize.

The second is uncertainty about other relevant decisions. As society grows more interactive and technologies become more complex, the interdependencies between organizations and other social units increase, and their respective values and decisions become a critical factor in each unit's decision environment.[35] This is the kind of uncertainty, for example, that makes it difficult to predict the financial viability of a project in a year's time, without anticipating the Federal Reserve's future decisions about the interest rate. Again, this type of uncertainty often makes the design and implementation of public programs in areas such as health, welfare, or education contingent on the results of the next election. The third kind of uncertainty relates to value judgments. This will be addressed in more detail when we discuss goals.

Some have even questioned the assumption, basic to any normative model of decision making, that outcomes are the results of deliberate choices. In organizations, the important decisions often seem to be imposed by outside circumstances, or are only recognized in retrospect as the product of a series of unrelated, apparently trivial choices. Responsible officials may try to avoid critical choices, where a mistake may risk their jobs or careers. Such decisions, when inescapable, may end up being made by oversight, as it were; this explains "the phenomenon in complex organizations of 'important' choices that often appear to just 'happen'."[36]

On following pages: "The Planning Process."

Source: R. Hedman, *Stop Me Before I Plan Again*, Chicago, IL: Planners Press (American Planning Association) 1981, pp. 10–15. Copyright permission (and plates) from Richard Hedman, San Francisco, CA.

A final problem confronting the "classic" rational decision-making model is the interdependence of goals and means. Since this is especially relevant to planning, the next section will address this question in more detail. But it would be well, even after the barrage of criticism presented above, not to give up on rationality completely. We will return to ask what the implications may be of rationality, its advantages and its limits, on our ideas of the decision making process.

Goals and Means

The rational approach to problem solving includes a prescribed relationship between goals and means. Goals must be set that provide the direction of the decision-making process and the framework for determining the ultimate choices. These goals derive, essentially, from the decision makers' basic norms and values, and may be quite general and abstract. They may be operationalized, therefore, as objectives that are specific targets of achievement or performance criteria.[37]

Goals, however, have turned out to be a concept that is elusive at best, and deceiving at worst. Moreover, the separate consideration of goals and means required by the rational model is dubious in theory and often impossible in practice. At one level of an organization goals may be set and objectives derived from them, which, for the next level up, may in fact be the means for accomplishing its goals. Thus, the goal of an organizational subunit may be a program element in the strategy devised by the organizations as a whole for meeting its goals. Conversely, what are defined as possible ways of accomplishing objectives set at a relatively high or abstract level of a decision-making, planning, or policymaking process, become the goals when these alternatives have to be elaborated for the more concrete levels below.

For example, a multidivisional corporation will have maximizing profit as its goal. In its situation this goal could require a mixed corporate strategy. Such strategy might demand increasing market penetration for one of its divisions, where opportunity beckons and competition seems soft, while for another division, faced with a less favorable environment, retrenchment and minimizing the cost of its product is more appropriate. Each of these roles, assigned to the divisions in the balance of overall corporate policy, becomes the division's goal.

Or, in the public sector, a city government might demand planning to improve the city's tax base. Means for reaching this objective might be enhancing the environment and opportunities in the city's business district, so as to attract commercial and service-related development, while for residential neighborhoods it might be to encourage preservation and rehabilitation for one, and to maximize development and new construction in another. Each of these objectives, in turn, becomes the goal by which the concrete alternatives for that sector are evaluated.

The problem lies in the complexity and infinite regress of this hierarchy of goals and means. To conform to the ideal norms of rationality, all these alternatives would have to be developed and evaluated simultaneously, down to the concrete level of implementation. Constraints of human behavior, limits of time, and resources clearly make this difficult, often impossible.[38] But if we limit ourselves to only part of this system, we run the risk of either developing abstract strategies that prove infeasible in practice, or selecting a particular course of concrete action that may turn out to be less than optimal in the light of higher-level goals.

Goal setting, then, is closely interdependent with the identification of alternative means. But it is also related to the appreciation of relevant constraints that delimit the decision space, and may in fact, leave very little flexibility indeed. As Simon paraphrased a familiar epigram: "If you allow me to determine the constraints, I don't care who selects the optimization criterion.[39]

Even if we agree on the need for goals as a standard of reference in evaluating alternative choices, another set of questions confronts us: Whose goals? Which goals? Goals when? Obviously, for an individual's own decisions these questions are trivial. But in trying to fathom the goals of a societal unit—a group, organization, or government—the answers to these questions are critical.[40] In determining an organization's objectives, for example, do we ask the management—the organization's "dominant elite"—or its clientele? Do we accept its aims as stated in speeches, reports, or legislation, or do we look for the deeper—perhaps more real—goals, which guide its actual behavior;[41] Can we assume that goals remain constant or must we take into account that values will probably change, especially over the long period of time between the conception of a plan and its implementation?[42]

These problems often have to be, and are, addressed in practice, and some helpful approaches have been developed. There are methods, such as "judgment analysis"[43] that make it easier for individuals to identify their own priorities. Other analytic techniques, such as "content analysis,"[44] which analyzes statements for their hidden or deeper meanings, or interactive approaches, like the "nominal group" method,[45] help in identifying group goals.

Nevertheless, whenever engaged in a planning endeavor based on the rational model, we have to remain conscious of the limitations and possible bias of the goals and objectives that guide the undertaking. One response to this realization has been a proposal for "directional" rather than goal-oriented planning.[46] This suggests that, rather than setting specific goals and objectives, the decision-making process merely point in a general "direction." However, in light of the interrelated hierarchy of goals, objectives, and means, and some of its difficulties which were discussed above, it is difficult to see what problems this proposal solves.

In fact, some observers question whether the problem-solving process is usually initiated on the perception of a problem: does decision making always begin with the identification of goals? Perhaps, they suggest, answers go looking for questions at least to the same extent that we imagine ourselves seeking solutions to problems.[47] For example, few firms perceived that they had information-processing problems, until they were offered computer technology which evolved in the 1950s.[48] The adoption of word-processing today is another case to illustrate how the prospect of resources may in itself create choices: solutions for problems that were not identified before these new opportunities became available.

Limitations to Rationality and Their Implications

We have seen that a good deal of the precedent research suggests that people and organizations rarely actually do make decisions rationally. If we are dealing here with a model designed for application in real-life situations, this in itself might be cause for pause. But many theorists and observers of the decision-making process have also accounted for why this has happened, suggesting that in real, rather than abstract contexts, decisions *cannot* be made as prescribed by the rational model.

As this realization dawned on planning theorists several responses evolved, which we shall briefly review. Practitioners, of course, intuitively knew and often acted out all along what has only gradually been "revealed" by research.[49] This is the basis, perhaps, for one response to the limitations of the formal model of rationality: the abandonment of theory, and the suggestion that practitioners, in fact, are making up theory as they go.[50] While this may be flattering to planners' egos, it deprives them of the kind of normative framework for analysis and actions that theory has traditionally provided.

Another response has been to examine more closely the relationship between decision making and its contexts.[51] This has undoubtedly enriched our appreciation of the complexities of the decision process. Some have attempted to build on this, and to combine some of the normative models discussed above in a contingent approach.[52] Such an approach aspires to tell decision makers in a given set of circumstances (which may conform to any of a number of set conditions) how they should make their choices: "If you are in situation A addressing problem type B, then do C."

Etzioni's "mixed scanning" is also a type of contingency approach. Here, rather than different contexts, the different contingencies are the various levels of decision making. Problem solving at the lower, more operational levels, Etzioni suggests, can be and is undertaken in the "incremental" mode, where choices are perceived to be constrained to alternatives not too different from the status quo. In addition to these "tactical" levels, however, there are higher levels, where decision makers have to be aware of the broader, more "strategic" picture. Organizations can, and should, "scan" their environments over a continuum of different levels, ranging from "tactical" operational issues to basic strategic choices. The latter, of course, while more critical, are also more rare, and in turn set the parameters that consttrain decision making relating to lower-level problems.[53]

Undoubtedly, this model has made a valuable contribution in resolving some of the contradictions between the rational and incremental approaches. A contingency theory perhaps offers the best promise of replacing the rational approach as a model for decision making that can combine operational prescriptions with situational realism. But the "mixed scanning" approach, and other contingency models that have been presented to date, still need a good deal of work and thought before they can fulfill this role.

Finally, some have suggested borrowing a substitute for traditional rationality from another field, such as philosophy. Philosophical models that have been offered include phenomenology and existentialism, both of which focus on actors' interpretation of and interaction with their contexts.[54] The problem with these approaches, however, is exactly that they are situation-specific; they say to the decision maker: you and your problem are unique. But what we are looking for is a model that is, if not universal, as the rational model claimed to be, at least more general, so that the official, planner, and analyst can identify their situation with a class of problems, and apply an available prescription to develop the best means for addressing it.

From the domains of philosophy and the sociology of knowledge comes another proposed substitute for the rational model. This is based on critical theory, a theory that sees social interactions as essentially a process of communication, and decision making as a matter of interpretation and enactment.[55] Critical theory offers a model that is certainly rich and realistic enough to have the potential of becoming the framework for a new approach to decision making and problem solving. It remains to be seen, however, whether this approach can extend beyond the conceptual and relatively general level, and is capable (as the rational model was thought to be) of generating concrete normative prescriptions capable of application in real-life situations.

Alternatively, some of the current descriptive decision models, such as "satisficing" and "incrementalism," have been proposed as new norms by their originators and others.[56] Frederickson calls this "buffered rationality," where commitments to short-term agreed-upon activities replace the systematic search for optimal choices to achieve identified goals, politics are integrated with planning, and "planning is closely wedded to action".[57] This resembles Gross' suggestion of "an action concept of rationality",[58] in response to the limitations of "classic" rationality. In a similar response, Friedmann also called for relating planning to action, and developed his model of "transactive planning," which calls for a much more personalized and interactive style of planning, organized primarily in small groups.[59]

Unfortunately, each of these proposals suffers from one defect or another when considering it as a replacement for the rational approach as a normative decision-making and planning model. Descriptive models such as "incrementalism" and "satisficing" have little to warrant their claim to normative value, apart from the fact that they are often used, and are feasible in many situations. No case is made for these approaches being a more logical way to make decisions than pure intuition, or for their being able to generate "good" decisions, or optimal choices, when applied. Modified forms of rationality, like Frederickson's "buffered rationality" or "directional planning" leave unclear how they will address the problems they are supposed to resolve, let alone how they are to be operationalized. This is true, too, for "transactive planning," which also assumes that all social problems can be addressed by small groups, an assumption that the imperatives of advanced technology have made untenable. Toxic waste disposal or satellite communications, to name just two of a multitude of similar issues, cannot be dealt with in intimate, "commune"-type organizations.

It is time to accept the limitations of the rational decision-making model. The empirical evidence that has accumulated, and the many valid objections that have been raised, remind one of the gathering weight of geological and paleontological findings that eroded the biblical theory of creation. But in the realm of planning and decision theory, we are still waiting for our Darwin, and for the counterpart to the theory of evolution.

Meanwhile, we must be aware that the rational model is not a realistic description of how decisions are made, and that it cannot be applied operationally without materially relaxing the assumptions that give it its validity. Thus, in the outcome, it becomes a matter of judgment whether the choice prescribed by "rational" analysis is, in fact, the optimal course of action.

However, as a normative model that prescribes how decisions can be made that conform to certain norms of logic and consistency, the rational model has yet to be superseded. Its usefulness has been repeatedly demonstrated as the underpinning for a series of practical analytic methods, while it continues to provide an essential vehicle for communicating the reasoning behind particular choices among people and groups who may not intuitively understand these decisions.

In the last three decades, there have been many proposals to modify or replace the rational model as the normative basis for decision making and problem solving in planning, management, administration, and policy analysis. Some of these proposals have made significant contributions, and a few offer promise of becoming an integrating framework for developing a new decision-making model in the future. But none can be confidently identified as *the* new normative decision model. Nor, indeed, have any of these theories gained widespread recognition or acceptance as a basis for practice although some of them have been around for many years.[60]

Though we may hope that the emergence of a new model is imminent, it is more likely that, for the forseeable future, planners will have to work with what they have. In their day-to-day practice, planners will continue to face the challenge of resolving the logical prescriptions of normative rationality with the pragmatic demands of their real-world environment.

Discussion Questions and Exercises

1. A. A group of systems analysts are trying to work out the optimum combination of hardware and software to serve the information-

processing needs of a medium-sized city's assessment, planning, and budgeting departments.

B. The planning department is working with the Mayor's office and the City Council to develop an effective system of allocating money received under the Community Development Block Grant program between neighborhood groups and community projects.

C. The State Bureau of Planning and Energy is reviewing the local electric utility company's application to site a new power plant, taking into account prospective costs of power generation and transportation to urban markets, and possible social, environmental, and ecological impacts.

D. A firm of planning consultants has been requested to advise a local hospital consortium and the city's department of human services on how many ambulances should be deployed and where to place their stations so as to minimize response times to calls.

Which of the above cases are exercises in instrumental rationality, and which demand substantive rationality? Give the reasons for your answers.

2. Which of the following sets of preferences are transitive and which are intransitive?

A. Atlanta > Baltimore; Baltimore > Cleveland; Atlanta > Cleveland; Baltimore > Detroit; Cleveland > Detroit; Atlanta > Detroit.

B. Atlanta > Baltimore; Detroit > Baltimore; Atlanta > Cleveland; Cleveland > Detroit; Atlanta > Detroit; Cleveland > Baltimore.

C. blue-striped neckties > red-polka-dotted ties;
   blue-striped ties > green striped ties;
   red-polka-dotted ties > green striped ties;
   green striped ties > blue-striped ties.

3. For each of the following cases, identify whether it is a situation of certainty, uncertainty, or risk. Give the reasons for each of your answers.

A. A game of blackjack.

B. Estimating what the American people think of the President's performance based on a sample survey.

C. Deciding whether to invest in a new manufacturing plant in a third world country, where previous changes in the government have sometimes resulted in nationalizations and expropriations.

D. Projecting a city's 1985 population based on available census data.

E. Deciding when to give his/her next birthday present to your closest living relative.

4. You have to choose in the morning between taking your umbrella to work or not. Which of the following factors is *irrelevant* for determining the utility, or value, of each of the possible courses of action:

   a. The cost of carrying the umbrella;
   b. The benefits of staying dry;
   c. The likelihood of rain;
   d. The cost of getting wet.

   What is the reason for your answer?

5. In the choice posed by the above question, if the chances of rain next day were 30%, what would be the other "state of nature" and its probability;

   a. The likelihood of being struck by lightning = 0.001%;
   b. The chance that there will be no rain = 70%;
   c. The chances that there may be sunshine = 70%;
   d. The likelihood of no rain = 75%.

6. Use the decision matrix method to decide whether to take your car to work tomorrow, ride your bicycle, or walk, where the relevant "states of nature" incorporate weather and traffic conditions:

   Alternative actions: (a) drive your car; (b) ride your bike; (c) walk.
   Alternative "states of nature": 1. heavy traffic/sunny (p = 0.6);
                                   2. light traffic/rain (p = 0.2);
                                   3. moderate traffic/cloudy (p = 0.2).
   Alternative outcomes and their utilities for you: (a)1: 5; (a)2: 10; (a)3: 8; (b)1: 2; (b)2: −10; (b)3: 10; (c)1: 10; (c)2: −10; (c)3: 6.

   What course of action would you choose under:

   A. The criterion of maximizing expected utility of the most probable outcome?
   B. The criterion of maximizing the sum of the expected utilities of a course of action?
   C. The "minimax" criterion?

   Which of these criteria (A, B, or C) is optimistic, pessimistic, or "neutral"? Is your decision "sensitive" to the decision criterion you choose?

If it is, to which, and why? How would you eventually choose a particular course of action?

7. Which of the following cases is an example of (a) rational decision-making; (b) "satisficing"; or (c) "disjointed incrementalism"; or a combination of these, and why?

A. In the face of an anticipated deficit, the governor and his budget bureau are deliberating on possible across-the-board budget cuts of 4%, 6%, or 8% of last year's allocations to all state agencies and departments. They finally decide on 6%, because this will come closest to eliminating the deficit, while not risking as much political "flak" as the 8% cut.

B. You are looking for a good used car, and have a budget of $2,500. You make your selection by identifying several reputable dealers and examining and pricing out the models you like. Each model you look at is either too expensive, or it has some critical defects. Eventually you find a car "you can live with," and though it is priced at $3,000, after bargaining the dealer agrees to sell for $2,750, and you buy.

C. A neighborhood organization is looking for a site for its proposed community center. It identifies all the available locations in the neighborhood that are large enough parcels to hold a building fitting the center's program and activities, and compares them for cost, relevant physical characteristics, and accessibility to neighborhood residents. It chooses the site that scores highest on a weighted score that reflects the selection committee's estimate of the relative importance of each of these considerations.

D. The city is looking for a new city manager. A search committee of elected and senior appointed officials draws up an advertisement specifying the appropriate qualifications, and advertises nationwide. Out of all the applicants, a short list is drawn up, who are then interviewed, but each of these lacks one essential qualification. However, finally the committee chooses the person who seems to come closest to meeting their specifications.

8. In terms of Arrow's criteria for rational collective choice, evaluate the process of choosing an American president. How rational and effective is it, and what would you recommend to bring it closer to meeting the standards for rational social choice?

Notes

1. G. C. Hemmens and B. Stiftel, "Sources for the Renewal of Planning Theory," *Journal of the American Planning Association*, 46(3) (July 1980): 345.

2. H. Baum, "Towards a Post-Industrial Planning Theory," *Policy Sciences* 8(4) (December 1977): 403-404.

3. K. Mannheim, *Man and Society in an Age of Reconstruction* (London: Kegan-Paul, 1947).

4. M. Weber *Economy and Society: An Outline of Interpretive Sociology I*, (G. Roth and C. Wittich, eds.), (New York: Bedminster Press, 1968), pp. 85-86.

5. *Ibid*, p. 26.

6. P. N. Levin *Government and the Planning Process* (London: Allen and Unwin, 1976), p. 225.

7. N. Lichfield, P. Kettle, and M. Whitbread, *Evaluation in the Planning Process* (Oxford: Pergamon, 1975), pp. 6-7.

8. J. Marschak, "Decision Making: Economic Aspects," *International Encyclopedia of the Social Sciences IV* (D. Sills, ed.) (New York: Macmillan, 1968), pp. 42-55.

9. C. H. Coombs, *A Theory of Data* (New York: Wiley, 1964), pp. 106-118.

10. S. Kassouf, *Normative Decision Making* (Englewood Cliffs, N.J.: Prentice-Hall, 1970).

11. J. V. Bradley, *Probability; Decision; Statistics* (Englewood Cliffs, N.J.: Prentice-Hall, 1976), pp. 68-89. K. J. Arrow and L. Hurwicz, "An Optimality Criterion for Decision Making Under Ignorance," *Uncertainty and Expectations in Economics: Essays in Honor of F. L.S. Shackle* (C. F. Carter and J. F. Ford, eds.) (Oxford: Blackwell, 1972), pp. 1-11.

12. W. Edwards, "Behavioral Decision Theory," *Annual Review of Psychology*, 12 (1961): 473-498.

13. M. Friedman and J. L. Savage, "The Utility Analysis of Choices Involving Risk," *Journal of Political Economy*, 56 (1948): 279-304.

14. I. D. J. Bross, *Design for Decision: An Introduction to Statistical Decision Making* (New York: Free Press, 1961), pp. 102-117.

15. E. J. Mishan, *Cost-Benefit Analysis* (2nd ed.) (London: G. Allen, 1971). G. H. Peters, *Cost-Benefit Analysis and Public Expenditure* (3rd ed.), (London: Institute of Economic Affairs, 1973). M. B. Teitz, "Cost-Effectiveness: A Systems Approach to the Analysis of Urban Services," *Journal of the American Institute of Planners* 34(3) (September 1968): 303-311. J. M. English (ed.), *Cost-Effectiveness: The Economic Evaluation of Engineered Systems*, (New York: Wiley, 1968). J. V. Bradley, *Analysis for Investment Decisions*, (London: Haymarket Press, 1974). S. J. Rosen, *Manual for Environmental Impact Evaluation* (Englewood Cliffs, N.J.: Prentice-Hall, 1976). R. W. Burchell and D. Listokin, *The Fiscal Impact Handbook: Projecting the Local Costs and Revenues Relating to Growth* (Rutgers University—Center for Urban Policy Research, 1978). D. Runyan, "Tools for Community-Managed Impact Assessment," *Journal of the American Institute of Planners*, 43(4) (April 1977): 125-134.

16. W. Alonso, "Predicting Best with Imperfect Data," *Journal of the American Institute of Planners* 34(2) (July 1968): 248-255.

17. K. J. Arrow, *Social Choice and Individual Values* (New York: Wiley, 1963).
18. E. I. Friedland and S. J. Cimbala, "Process and Paradox: The Significance of Arrow's Theorem," *Theory and Decision*, 4(1) (September 1973): 51-64.
19. M. Olson, *The Logic of Collective Action: Public Goods and the Theory of Groups* (Cambridge, Mass.: Harvard University Press, 1965).
20. A. J. Catanese, *Planners and Local Politics: Impossible Dreams* (Beverly Hills, Calif.: Sage, 1974).
21. R. P. Mack, *Planning on Uncertainty: Decision Making in Business and Government Administration* (New York: Wiley-Interscience, 1971), pp. 71, 175-249. G. Zaltman, R. Duncan, and J. Holbeck, *Innovations and Organizations*, (New York: Wiley-Interscience, 1973), pp. 53-58.
22. H. A. Simon, *Models of Man, Social and Rational* (New York: Wiley, 1957).
23. C. E. Lindblom, "The Science of Muddling Through," *Public Administration Review*, 19 (1959): 59-88. D. Braybrooke and C. E. Lindblom, *A Strategy of Decision: Policy Evaluation as a Social Process* (Glencoe, Ill.: Free Press, 1963).
24. P. A. Phyrr, "Zero-Base Budgeting," *Public Administration Review*, 37(1) (January-February 1977): 1-8.
25. A. Wildavsky, *The Politics of the Budgetary Process* (Boston, Mass.: Little-Brown, 1964).
26. O. A. Davis, M. A. H. Dempster, and A. Wildavsky, "A Theory of the Budgetary Process," *American Political Science Review*, 60(3) (September 1966). G. C. Edwards III and I. Sharkansky, *The Policy Predicament: Making and Implementing Public Policy* (San Francisco, Calif.: Freeman, 1978).
27. J. J. Bailey and R. J. O'Connor, "Operationalizing Incrementalism: Measuring the Muddles," *Public Administration Review* 35(1) (January-February 1975): 60-66. L. T. LeLoup and W. B. Moreland, "Agency Strategies and Executive Review: The Hidden Politics of Budgeting," *Public Administration Review* 38(3) (May-June 1978): 232-239. J. E. Skok, "Budgetary Politics and Decision Making: Development of an Alternative Hypothesis for State Government," *Administration and Society*, 11(4) (February 1980): 445-460.
28. E. R. Alexander, "Choice in a Changing World," *Policy Sciences*, 3(3) (September 1972): 325-337.
29. K. A. Archibald, "Three Views of the Expert's Roles in Policymaking: Systems Analysis, Incrementalism, and the Clinical Approach," *Policy Sciences*, 1(1) (Spring 1970): 76.
30. Y. Dror, "Muddling Through—Science or Inertia," *Public Administration Review*, 24.
31. J. D. Steinbrenner, *The Cybernetic Theory of Decision: New Dimensions of Political Analysis* (Princeton, N.J.: Princeton University Press, 1974).
32. N. E. Long, "The American Administrator in Modern Complex Society," in *Empathy and Ideology* (C. Press and A. Arian, eds.) (Chicago, Ill.: Rand McNally, 1966).
33. P. Hall, *Great Planning Disasters*, (London: Weidenfeld & Nicholson, 1980), pp. 6-11, 15-151, 250-253.
34. J. K. Friend and W. N. Jessop, *Local Government and Strategic Choice*, (London: Tavistock Publications, 1969).

35. S. Terreberry, "The Evolution of Organizational Environments," *Administrative Science Quarterly*, 12(4) (September 1968): 590–613.
36. M. D. Cohen and J. G. March, *Leadership and Ambiguity: The American College President*, (New York: McGraw-Hill, 1974), p. 86.
37. Lichfield, Kettle, and Whitbread, op. cit., pp. 22–30.
38. E. C. Banfield, "Ends and Means in Planning," *International Social Science Journal*, 11(3) (March 1959):
39. H. A. Simon, "On the Concept of Organizational Goal," *Administrative Science Quarterly*, 9(2) (June 1964): 6.
40. R. T. Hall, "Effectiveness Theory and Organizational Effectiveness," *Journal of Applied Behavioral Science*, 16(4) (October-December, 1980): 536-545. W. R. Scott, "Effectiveness of Organizational Effectiveness Studies," in *New Perspectives on Organizational Effectiveness*, P. S. Goodman, J. M. Pennings & Assocs., (San Francisco, Calif.: Jossey-Bass, 1977).
41. A. Etzioni, *Modern Organizations* (Englewood Cliffs, N.J.: Prentice-Hall, 1964), pp. 6-7. C. Perrow, "The Analysis of Goals in Complex Organizations," *American Social Science Review*, 26(6) (December 1961): 854-865.
42. G. Vickers, "Values, Norms and Policy," *Policy Sciences* 4(1) (March 1973): 103-112.
43. T. R. Stewart and L. Gelberd, "Analysis of Judgment Policy: A New Approach for Citizen Participation in Planning," *Journal of the American Institute of Planners*, 42(1) (January 1976): 33-41.
44. C. Krippendorff, *Content Analysis: An Introduction to its Methodology*, (Beverly Hills, Calif.: Sage, 1980).
45. A. L. Delbecq, A. H. Van de Ven, and D. H. Gustafson, *Group Techniques for Program Planning: A Guide to Nominal Group and Delphi Processes*, (Glenview, Ill.: Scott Foresman & Co., 1975).
46. M. B. McCaskey, "A Contingency Approach to Planning: Planning With Goals and Planning Without Goals," *Academy of Management Journal*, 17(2) (June 1974): 281-291.
47. M. D. Cohen, J. G. March and J. P. Olson, "A Garbage Can Model of Organizational Choice," *Administrative Science Quarterly*, 17(1) (March 1972): 1-
48. A. Pettigrew, *The Politics of Organizational Decision Making*, (London: Tavistock Publications, 1973).
49. A. J. Catanese, op. cit.
50. D. A. Schon, "Some of What a Planner Knows: A Case Study of Knowing-in-Practice," *Journal of the American Planning Associates* 48(3) (Summer 1982): 351-364.
51. Steinbrunner, op. cit.
52. B. M. Hudson, "Comparison of Current Planning Theories: Counterparts and Contradictions... T. D. Galloway, "Comments," *Journal of the American Planning Assoc.*, 45(4) (October 1979): 387-403.
53. A. Etzioni, "Mixed Scanning: A "Third" Approach to Decision-Making," *Public Administration Review*, 27 (December 1967): 385-392.
54. M. Krieger, "Some New Directions for Planning Theories," *Journal of the American Institute of Planning*, 40(3) (May 1974): 156-163. J. Forester, "Crit-

55. J. Forester, "Questioning and Organizing Attention: Toward a Critical Theory of Planning and Administrative Practice," *Administration and Society* 13 (1981): 161-205.
56. E. C. B. Schoettle, "The State of the Art in Policy Studies," in *The Study of Policy Formation* (R. Bauer and K. J. Gergen, eds.), (New York: Free Press, 1968).
57. H. G. Frederickson, "Public Administration in the 1970's: Development and Direction," *Public Administration Review*, 36(5) (September-October 1976): 569-570.
58. B. Gross, "Planning in an Era of Social Revolution," *Public Administration Review*, 31(3) (May-June 1971): 259-296, p. 293.
59. J. Friedmann, *Retracking America*, (New York: Anchor-Doubleday, 1973).
60. E. R. Alexander, "After Rationality, What? A Review of Responses to Paradigm Breakdown," *Journal of the American Planning Association*, 50(1) (Winter, 1984): 62-69; see also *Rationality in Planning: Critical Essays on The Role of Rationality in Urban and Regional Planning*, (M. Braheny and A. Hooper, eds.), (London: Pion, 1985).

CHAPTER 3

What and How? Planning Definitions and Process

There is some connection, as we have seen, between planning and the rational decision-making process. But are they identical? What, in fact, is planning, and what is the planning process? These, again, are questions to which there is no single agreed-upon answer. Below, we will explore the range of current thinking, and see whether we can arrive at any acceptable synthesis.

Definitions: What is Planning?[1]

Over twenty years ago John Dyckman referred to the discussion of this question as "a literature of controversy." More recently, Henry Hightower said: "The 'Square One' question is: what is planning?"[2] Clearly, not much has changed. But perhaps we can mine a synthesis out of an exploration of the views of planning that have emerged over the years.

One view sees planning as a basic activity pervading human behavior at the individual and every social level. In this view, "planning is a process. . . of human thought and action based upon that thought—in point of fact, forethought. . .which is a very general human activity."[3] In their analysis of the planning components of human behavior, George Miller and others concluded that every action is the result of a complex process, of which planning is an integral part.[4]

This approach gives planning a universality that may help disabuse planners of the notion that they are engaged in some esoteric activity. At the same time, it does not preclude the possibility of expertise. But the broad sweep of this definition is also its major flaw: if planning is an integral part of all human activity, what is there to distinguish it or to warrant giving planning any particular attention?

A hardly narrower definition is offered by Moore, who suggests that: "All those making decisions about the allocation and distribution of public resources are, in fact, planning."[5] This definition enables the justification of planning, in the course of legitimating any appropriate public intervention. So, for example, planning becomes appropriate to avoid externalities (the smell of the tannery in the adjoining residential suburb) or to provide public goods, such as highways and schools.

But this view of planning suffers from imprecision, as Moore admits. Is the council member who is a member of the local authority's parks committee, or the member of Congress who sits on the Environment Committee, a planner? And is what they do planning, more than the development of exploration and investment policy by Exxon, policy that, in determining the location, expansion or phase-out of major oil wells, refineries, and terminals, will directly affect the employment of thousands of people and may have significant long-term impact on the economies of regions and nations?

A second approach to defining planning emphasizes its anticipatory nature, and equates planning with "foresight in formulating and implementing programs and policies,"[6] or "advance laying out of a program of actions."[7] The future orientation of planning may also be stressed,[8] but, as Ozbekhan concedes for this kind of definition (which includes his own): "What we call planning. . .enters into any rational human action system."[9] A definition that is so broad is obviously of limited value.

A third view claims that: "In general, planning is a procedure for arranging beforehand, by deliberately sequencing actions so as to achieve an objective. . ."[10] or it is "a process for determining appropriate future actions through a sequence of choices."[11] Little distinguishes this idea of planning from the rational decision-making process, except, perhaps, a clearer future orientation. Again, this definition does not enable us to distinguish planning from other components of behavior or action that are not planning.

Wildavsky's definition of planning, as the control of future action, focuses on another flaw in the previous definitions, and tries to compensate for it. This is their failure to link planning with action; consequently, Wildavsky points out, these definitions provide no criteria for planning evaluation.

The link between planning and action leads critics such as Wildavsky to conclude that planning is limited by our capacity to control future outcomes. Advocates of planning-as-control also reject any divorce of planning from implementation, but they characterize this as a failure of nerve. John Friedman proposes a model of planning that "fuses action and planning," saying:

> it is possible to assert that any action that is deliberate is also to a certain degree planned. The problem is no longer how to make decision more "rational," but how to improve the quality of the action.[12]

Definitions linking planning with action, however, have the same flaws of generality as the "basic human activity" and "rational choice" models. Is one planning when one pays the telephone bill, a decision that influences the future actions of the telephone company? If so, the concept of planning becomes so diluted as to be devoid of any real meaning. Or, in another sense, it may set standards so high that they are impossible to meet.

Besides such process-oriented definitions of planning, there are more situational definitions. Such views focus less on what planning does and how it does it and more on planning's aims and its domain. One opinion is that planning is problem solving that is aimed at very particular kinds of problems, "wicked problems." These are problems that have no definitive formulations, no clear rules, no "true-or-false" answers (they can only be "better" or "worse"), and no clear test for the solution.[13]

Hightower expresses a similar view, but extends planning beyond "wicked problems." His definition accounts for planners' tendencies to question values, institutions, and given rules, and their use of rough, imprecise data. But this approach, as is beginning to seem almost inevitable, is also too inclusive. True, planners are familiar with "wicked problems," messy data, and want to see their proposals implemented, but the same can be said of politicians, administrators, and entrepreneurs.

One definition that does not suffer from the ills of inclusiveness is that of Sir Geoffrey Vickers. For Vickers, planning is what planners do.[14] Unquestionably, this pragmatic approach has the merits of being simple and intuitively obvious. But if planners are merely people who plan, we are left with a tautology and are back where we started: without a definition that is capable of telling us at once what planning is and distinguishing it from what planning is not.

If I join this long line of definers, it is in the hope that their contributions will at least preclude some types of possible errors. Previous definitions were too careful, perhaps, not to exclude any aspect of planning. As a result, they ended up as almost all-inclusive. Perhaps it will be useful to adopt the opposite approach and begin by identifying what planning is not.

If we consider planning as a process or activity that is the framework for a profession or semiprofession, which lays claims to being a discipline, and which is oriented toward social decisions and public policy,[15] then some distinctions between planning and nonplanning activities can be readily made.

First, planning is not a purely individual activity. Indeed, it is done by individuals, but it is done in order to affect the actions of groups, organizations, or government. Planning for personal actions exists too, but it should be distinguished from planning in the societal sense, with which we are concerned here.

Nor is planning present-oriented. How far into the future plans can reasonably be projected as worth discussing.[16] But in every case, planning is concerned with future actions involving a significant element of uncertainty. Consequently planning involves both predictions of, and control over, outcomes.

Planning cannot be routinized. Many problems are not unique, and these can be attacked with existing solutions or problem-solving algorithms.[17] These, however, are the polar opposites of the typical problems that are the objects of planning efforts. This distinction is useful when we attempt to separate the apparent from the real planning activity in institutional settings. Development administrators, for example, may do their jobs in a planning agency, but if they are only applying existing regulations and controls they are doing very little or no planning.

Planning has little or nothing in common with trial-and-error approaches to problem solving. This is not to say that planning cannot incorporate experiments in a limited way, but this will be in the context of a deliberately conceived strategy. Decision making based on incremental trials and comparison, as formalized in Lindblom's "disjointed incrementalism," is not planning. In fact, this approach has been described as "nonplanning."[18]

Planning is not just the imagining of desirable futures. The distinction between planning and utopian thinking is just as important as a sense of their relationship: "Planning, like utopia, depicts a desirable future state of affairs, but, unlike utopia, specifies the means for achieving it."[19] Thinking about strategies for social change without intending to implement them, or without the power to carry them out, may be productive, but it is not planning. Philosophers such as Rousseau, historians such as Marx, economists such as Mill and Keynes, or more recently, Galbraith or Friedman, have had effects on society that are sometimes profound and have clearly influenced the policies of governments. But their theories were not plans, and their only implementation tool was the power of persuasion.

Finally, planning is not just making plans. The link between planning and action, expressed in Wildavsky's definition, and reflected in an increasing concern with implementation, is now generally recognized.[20] Planning, then, to be worthy of the name, must include the commitment and the power—at least, by an a priori estimate, though of course this may be refuted by the lesson of experience—to carry out the planned strategies, actions, projects, or programs to successful conclusion.

If planning is not an individual activity, not present-oriented, not routinized, not trial-and-error, not utopian, and not limited to plan making, what is it? It must be societal, future-oriented, nonroutinized, deliberate, strategic, and linked to action.

To synthesize these terms in a definition, I propose that planning is the deliberate social or organizational activity of developing an optimal strategy of future action to achieve a desired set of goals, for solving novel problems in complex contexts, and attended by the power and intention to commit resources and to act as necessary to implement the chosen strategy.

The Planning Process

Doubts about the possibility of generalizing about planning are reflected in the multiplicity of planning models that have been developed. At some level of abstraction, more removed from the complexities of real-world contexts, generalization may be possible. Such generalization takes the form of models, which have been developed by many students of the planning process, such as Banfield, Friend, and Jessop, and Lichfield.[21]

There has already been mention of how much the planning process resembles the decision-making process in general. Decision-making models like Mack's DOSRAP (deliberative-ongoing-staged-recursive-administrative-process)[22] or Stokey and Zeckhauser's policy analysis model[23] are quite like the planning process that will be described below in their essential aspects. Again, however, a caveat: the fact that the planning or decision-making process is often abstracted in a certain way is no guarantee that this is the way, in fact, that these processes actually play themselves out when real live people are planning or making decisions. Some research, indeed, suggests that this is not so.[24]

While differing in some specifics and terminology, all these models have one thing in common. They see planning as a sequential, multistaged process in which many of the phases are linked to their predecessors by feedback loops. In other words, the conclusions reached at a later stage may lead to a review of an earlier stage or a reiteration of the whole process. For example, an agency may find that all the alternatives that have been developed to meet certain objectives are too expensive. It may discover in its evaluation (later stage) that none of them is feasible. This is bound to cause a reappraisal of the goals and objectives decided upon at an earlier stage of planning. Or the monitoring and evaluation of the impacts of plans or programs may reveal new problems, which become the stimulus for a new round of planning.

The following major components of the planning process tend to be found in most models of the planning process.

Problem Diagnosis

Planning begins, like the decision process, with some sense of a dissatisfaction with the status quo; if there were no problem, there would be no need for action. The diagnosis of the problem depends on an image of the desired state, which acts as the point of reference. The image gives form to specific goals, general norms, standards, ideologies, even utopian visions.

Problem diagnosis, in the institutional setting in which most planning takes place, may already be largely completed when the planners or analysts receive their brief. Their assignment may, in itself, set quite determinate bounds to alternative ways in which the problem can be perceived. So, for example, the way their assignment was presented to planners for the Roskill Commission was identifying the best site for a third London airport, though, in fact, the commission's charge also gave it the latitude to consider whether an airport would be needed at all. This case shows how important it is for planners to review the way the problem is defined in their charge, and where appropriate, to make the case for amending their terms of reference.

Naturally, in many cases problems are not defined so clearly, and the planners' task includes diagnosis prior to developing alternative solution strategies. Members of a team engaged in developing revitalization proposals for a neighborhood, for example, have to collect and analyze data on past aspects of the neighborhood's development, and project what might occur in the future without their intervention, in order to identify the factors responsible for the area's decline, and thus focus their revitalization proposals on its basic problems.

Even a manifest crisis demanding action might only be a symptom of any of a number of different underlying problems that have to be identified before appropriate responses can be devised. Health planners in a hospital faced with dropping demand for its services, for instance, would have to review information on the costs and quality of services provided, demographic and sociocultural factors affecting demand, and the hospital's competitive and regulatory environment, to determine whether the problem was reduced need, increased competition, or any one of a host of other possibilities.

The definition of the problem aims the thrust of the solution. Definitions, however, depend on the analytical orientation of the individuals involved:

> The academic expert says to the client: "If the shoe fits, wear it.";
> The strategic expert says: "The shoe you're wearing doesn't fit, and you should try one like this instead."; and the clinical expert says: "If the shoe doesn't fit, then there's something wrong with your foot."[25]

The effect of role and professional or disciplinary background on problem definition is not limited, as one might think, to "soft" areas such as planning or developing policy. It extends to fields that appear completely objective, even to apparently "hard" science.[26]

The planner's role and ideological paradigms will also color definitions of problems. For example, viewing the poor as primarily responsible for their condition is bound up with a preference for a social services strategy against poverty. When social forces are viewed as the main cause of poverty, suggestions for structural change are not far behind.[27] This is just one example to illustrate how our problem definitions are linked to our assumed theories of human behavior. Such theories may often be implicit or subconscious, but the direction in which they bias our problem definitions may have a powerful effect on the ultimate planning or policy proposals.[28]

46 APPROACHES TO PLANNING

Empirical studies of how people go about problem definition that go beyond this type of anecdotal-introspective evidence are rare. Those that exist, however, suggest an intimate connection between context, style of enquiry, and problem perception,[29] on the one hand, and the location and availability of solutions on the other.[30]

Goal Articulation

Goals, as we have seen, relate to problem definitions. Planning was traditionally much more goal-oriented than it is now. City planning often meant little more than the development of a "master plan," which showed a desired end-state, in future year X, with the attainment of certain goals.

One of the most difficult challenges in planning is the translation of vague, incoherent goals into operational objectives; when this is not done, serious dysfunctions may result.[31] While there have been many attempts to develop technical means for goal articulation, the undertaking remains more of an art than a science.[32]

Nevertheless, the correct identification and clear articulation of goals and objectives are an important—perhaps a critical—part of the planning process. Clearly expressed goals are not only necessary to carry out the following stages of planning, such as alternatives' design and evaluation (see below), they are often also a significant element of the plan or policy itself, and their effective communication is regarded by many authorities as a major factor in whether a plan, policy, or program is successfully implemented.[33]

Like problem definition, planners in an organizational setting might be working, on a particular project, toward goals that are already given. In developing or reviewing proposals for development of a central business area, for instance, a city's planners might be explicitly directed to select the project that will have the most positive fiscal impact on the city: maximize its property tax base and increase its direct and indirect revenues while keeping the city's costs to a minimum. On the other hand, there are many situations where goals have to be articulated, by interaction with affected groups and individuals, or by analysis of relevant documents, and determined or inferred by the planners and analysts themselves.

Often, too, planners are faced with incompatible objectives. In trying to identify sites for low-income housing in one Western town, for example, the city's planners were confronted with two conflicting goals. On the one hand, the "best" sites could be those that would enable the construction of as much housing as possible with the funds available. On the other hand, the most appropriate locations would be those which would enhance socioeconomic and racial integration. The sites promoting the first objective were all in the town's black and poor neighborhoods: here the funds could be stretched, because the land was cheap. The second goal could only be achieved by locating the housing in white middle-class areas, but here the number of dwellings that could be built would be cut to half, because of the cost of land.

Of course, identifying goals and objectives may not be easy. In complex organizations and institutions, goal articulation may only be achieved through intensive negotiations, bargaining, and even conflict. Some keen observers of decision making in such contexts, such as Lindblom, suggest that this is one reason why rational, "synoptic" planning is avoided, and piecemeal "incremental" decision making is adopted instead.[34] In many situations this is probably true, and it poses a paradox for proponents of rational planning and decision making, which seems difficult to resolve.

One kind of resolution involves a compromise with incrementalism, the kinds of "buffered rationality" proposed by Frederickson[35] or "planning without goals" suggested by McCaskey[36] mentioned before. Another kind of resolution involves recognizing that incremental decision making may work in some kinds of situations that are so stable and structured that minor adjustments or adaptations in the routinized status quo are enough to address and resolve any problems. Here its goals are implicit in an organization's or institution's basic functions, structure, procedures, and domain, and their explicit invocation is unnecessary. However, such situations are not universal, and, indeed, perhaps they are becoming increasingly rare.[37] Where, instead of a structured status quo, decision makers encounter a situation of turbulence and flux—a new organization, a changing environment, novel problems, or a crisis which has resisted (or is itself the result of) routine attempts to overcome it—they have no option but to decide, often quite explicitly, where the organization has to go. This may demand leadership and claim a cost in personal interaction, even conflict, but the pain of goal articulation cannot always be avoided.

Prediction and Projection

Future orientation was emphasized in the definition of planning. This means that current data are not enough. The development of alternative solutions to problems always requires projection into the future in order to estimate the conditions, needs, and constraints.

Public works are an extreme case. The California Water Plan required over twenty years lead time. Utility companies commonly allow several years before implementation can begin, and they usually estimate a project or program life of several decades.

Prediction is essential for evaluating and selecting alternatives. Evaluation cannot be done without projecting the impacts of alternative proposals under possible future conditions. Can we predict the future? Yes, to a certain extent, but our success will depend upon the amount of information available and the continuity of the phenomenon being analyzed. Numerous population projections have been made, with an enviable record of success. Yet the U.S. Census Bureau erred in its estimates of 1970 population. The estimates were based on projections of previous trends, and changes in lifestyles that affected marriage and fertility between 1960 and 1970 were not anticipated.

A repertoire of predictive and projective techniques has been developed for different situations of information and uncertainty. There are methods such as curve fitting and shift-and-share analysis, which basically take quantitative observations of past trends and extrapolate them. There are more qualitative approaches, involving understanding and projection of various factors involved in historical processes, such as latent-factors analysis and scenario writing. Tools have also been developed for using experts' subjective knowledge to generate information about the future, such as the Delphi consultation technique.[38]

In planning, prediction and projection have two main aspects. We need to predict the future in order to estimate demand for facilities and services, and to assess our capacity to meet projected needs. Population and employment projections are used for this type of prediction. Also employed may be a wide variety of technology-related assessments, such as estimates of future rates of automobile ownership, which are critical in estimating the need for future highway construction, or projections of expected energy demand, basic to determining the future need for generating capacity. The other aspect of prediction is foreseeing the outcomes and impacts of alternative proposals, in order properly to evaluate them. One way of doing this is extrapolating, with appropriate modifications, from similar experiences in the past. Another is to try to simulate the effects of actions on their relevant environment by modeling their essential interactions. Computer simulation of the result of alternative highway configurations is an example of this approach.

"Design" of Alternatives[39]

We do not usually think of design when considering the planning process. Rather, design is commonly associated with giving form to some concrete response to a need or problem: a building (architectural design), a tool or product (product design), a machine or structure (engineering design), or a built environment of avenues or plazas (urban design). This view sees design as "to conceive the idea and prepare a description of a proposed system, artifact or aggregation of artifacts."[40] It only takes on step up the ladder of abstraction, however, to recognize design as a stage in the decision-making process: "everyone designs who devises courses of action aimed at changing existing situations into preferred ones."[41]

Design in the form-giving, or space-shaping sense—the sense in which it is commonly understood, and practiced by the other "design professions" of architecture, landscape architecture, engineering, industrial and product design—is a subset of alternatives' design at the more abstract level as defined here. Traditionally, however, while design in architecture, engineering, physical planning, and urban design has been well understood, its role in policy-oriented planning and related activities such as policy analysis, management, and administration has been ignored.

For planning, in particular, this is surprising, because planning is also one of the "design professions." This description perhaps owes more to the profession's original roots in civic architecture and municipal engineering.[42] But it does not seem unwarranted when we recognize that: "planning is *the design of the actions* which will change the object (of planning) in the manner that has been previously defined."[43] Indeed, the capability of designing alternative solutions ought to be one of the planner's unique skills, distinguishing us from more exclusively analytic practitioners such as policy analysts and systems analysts. The design of alternatives is as essential to planning as it is an integral part of decision making. A good plan must include deliberate design and cannot simply analyze given options: "A design of a good new alternative is likely to be worth a lot more than a thorough evaluation of some unsatisfactory old alternatives."[44]

What is design? The balance of available evidence suggests that design is a mix of search and creativity, and that creativity itself includes at least some, if not a good deal of, information retrieval, processing, and transformation.[45] However, there is probably at least a residue of inexplicable, extrarational creativity in addressing novel problems, nonroutine situations, or in developing highly innovative and unprecedented solutions.[46]

The design of alternative proposals in planning can take many different forms, depending on the nature of the issue or problem. Planners required to develop an EIS (environmental impact statement) for a proposed facility such as a power plant, or a solid waste disposal site, have to develop and evaluate alternatives as part of the EIS. Such alternatives might include other locations for the same or a similar facility. They could also describe different configurations of the plant, such as different sizes related to different projected capacity-requirement scenarios, which might even include not doing anything at all.

Another case might have an analyst required to develop a response to a policy issue: how to stimulate central city development, for example. Such a response will also demand the development of alternative courses of action. These could be designed on any of a number of different dimensions, such as city agency (assessor's office: delay reassessments, develop tax-increment finanacing area; zoning administrator: facilitate mixed and adaptive reuses by developing performance zoning codes, etc.) or implementation tool (taxes: tax increment financing, selective property tax abatements; funding: assist qualified developers and businesses with city revenue bonds, etc.). In short, virtually every type of planning or policy related assignment includes a "design" component, whether explicitly, as in the last example, or implicitly, as in the case of the EIS, which, on the face of it, is simply describing and analyzing the impact of a given proposal.

How can the rational elements of the design process be incorporated in systematic planning? Heuristic search is probably the most common aid to design in decision making today.[47] Heuristic search uses rules of thumb such as: "ask the fellow in the next office," "call up my old professor and ask her for some source of information on that subject," or: "look up the index of the nearest relevant professional journal." Unquestionably, planners' design abilities could be improved with more familiarity with the principles and practice of effective heuristic search.[48] Systematic search, consisting of deliberate information discovery and retrieval from sources ranging from in-house personnel, through outside experts and informants, to programmed search of data banks, is also still relatively neglected. When systematic search is applied to problem representations, it merges with design methods.

The introduction of systematic design methods into planning and policy making offers perhaps the greatest potential for enhancing the quality and range of alternatives.[49] This potential, however, is largely unrealized, since most existing design methods were developed for use in formal design tasks in engineering, product design, and architecture. As tools for articulating the dimensions of a problem or issue, and enabling identification of solution-related system variables, design methods, intelligently applied, can generate a broader and more innovative array of alternative solutions than unaided intuition or tradition-bound expertise.

There are some design methods that are suitable for planning and policy related applications. They include AIDA (analysis of interrelated decision areas),[50] the "morphological box,"[51] the IDEALS concept,[52] "idealized design,"[53] and IBIS (issue-based information systems).[54] Unfortunately, their diffusion and adoption in planning contexts is very limited, and examples of systematic design applications to policy problems are rare.[55]

Plan Testing

Before it is evaluated, each option that has been developed or designed has to be subjected to another test: is it internally consistent? And, is it feasible? The test for internal consistency examines each alternative solution and asks: does this proposal in fact respond to the objectives and constraints that have been set for it?[56] Sometimes in the design process one of a set of multiple objectives is lost sight of, or an important constraint is ignored. Cost overruns are a classic example of this phenomenon. When a proposal is quoted at 200% of its earlier estimated cost, sometimes after a considerable investment in detailed planning and design, planners are faced with the difficult decision of whether to modify this constraint or go back to the drawing board.

Feasibility analysis asks about each alternative proposal: Can it be done, given known constraints and available or projected resources? If the alternatives were well-designed, the answer will be affirmative. But negative answers may reduce the range of options to a short list, to only one alternative or to none. In the last case, the planners will have to re-design some options to make them feasible, or possibly even reassess their original objectives and goals.

Plan testing takes different forms in different contexts. The form with which we are, of course, most familiar, is pricing our proposals to see whether they meet cost constraints. More sophisticated versions of this include the cash-flow projections and financial analyses conventionally carried out for any real estate investment project. Other elements of plan testing for physical development proposals may include compatibility with topographic and site constraints, availability of appropriate services with adequate capacities, and minimum access to supply sources and markets.

Constraints on implementation are easy to identify when they are considered, but too often this is ignored until it is too late. The obvious constraints are economic and physical, like the ones described above. Less tangible constraints may also make a proposal infeasible. Some of these may be organizational, such as the absence of appropriate legal powers or statutory authority for a governmental unit to carry out a proposal, or the unavailability of appropriate personnel or suitably qualified contractors.[57] Others may be political: the opposition of an agency whose approval is critical, or the absence of support from staff whose cooperation is essential. The vested interest of an elected or appointed official, even, can be an insurmountable barrier: a development project requiring razing the house of the alderman chairing the Finance Committee is unlikely to get very far. All these factors, then, should be assessed in testing whether a proposal is, in fact, realistic or not.

Evaluation

The evaluation stage begins when the planners have a number of alternatives they know can be implemented. Which of them shall they implement? If there is only one alternative, there must be a "go/no-go" decision, either to carry out the proposed set of actions or to do nothing. This approach puts a strain on the analytic capacities of those involved because the absolute magnitude of effects becomes important.[58]

In other contexts, they know that something is going to be done, and they just have to choose the preferred alternative. With options to compare, the decision makers have some freedom to estimate the relative impact of each. It is important to remember, too, that one option is always to do nothing, and retain the status quo. Though on the face of it this situation comprises the problem to which alternative solutions are being sought, it is possible that, on sober evaluation, the status quo may turn out to be preferable, after all, to any feasible alternative course of action. Also, the situation "as is" is the datum against which each of the other alternatives must be evaluated.[59]

Which alternative do they like most? What does each of these options do for them? The answers to these questions depend on the evaluation criteria adopted. A commonly used criterion is efficiency: which alternative gives the "biggest bang for the buck?" Benefit-cost analysis, an evaluation method used extensively since it was developed in the 1950s, explicitly addresses this criterion.

Benefit-cost analysis is based upon the theory that the selection of a project or program should be determined by its net contribution to the economy or to some clearly specified economic unit. It applies the economic concept of marginality, meaning that the most efficient proposal is the one generating the greatest benefits for each unit of investment: this contribution is expressed in a benefit-to-cost ratio. The benefit-cost ratio expresses total benefits generated by a given option, in money, over its total costs.[60]

One of the advantages of benefit-cost analysis is that all the outputs must be quantified in money:

> Because in the public sector one is dealing with a budget constraint, comparisons are ideally made in dollar terms. Program alternatives that each have different measures of effectiveness essentially are impossible to compare. For example, how does one compare a reduction in the incidence of mortality from cancer with better education achieved by minorities through preschool head-start programs?[61]

However, this is also one of its greatest drawbacks. Imagine the problems in the above example. How do you put a value on lives saved, or on the benefits conferred by a better education—apart from a higher income? Nevertheless, benefit-cost analysis is a frequently used evaluation tool, because of its value as a framework for aggregating a broad range of outcomes for differing options into a single indicator that decision makers can intuitively understand.

When outcomes cannot easily be expressed in monetary values, as in human services, for example, such as day-care or mental health treatment, cost-effectiveness analysis may be used. This is a method that allows the evaluation and comparison of programs with similar outputs without converting those outputs into money. The programs are evaluated in terms of an output or effectiveness indicator, which is expressed as units of output per dollar cost.[62]

The utility of cost-effectiveness analysis in program evaluation is limited to comparing programs or services with similar outputs. It offers no way to aggregate the outputs of different types of programs (for example, a driver education program to promote the use of safety belts and a day care program for handicapped children) into a common, comparable denominator. It also is difficult to interpret the findings in any absolute sense. For example, it will be clear that a tutorial program delivering a 20% improvement in reading scores over a year per $1,000 spent is better than one delivering only a 10% improvement per $1,000, but it still is not obvious that either of these programs is a good investment of public money.

Another format for evaluating alternative proposals has to be employed when it becomes too difficult or prohibitively costly in time and analytic resources to quantify and aggregate their outputs. A way of formalizing and displaying these outputs is impact analysis. Impact analysis uses a matrix and some type of scoring system to indicate the relative value, utility, or disbenefit of each particular output and impact in the context of the particular evaluation. The factors to be taken into account in such analyses will vary according to the issue involved: The social impact of relocating a village from a plain that will be flooded by a proposed dam requires quite different analytic dimensions from the fiscal impact of a proposed municipal policy to abate property taxes on certain kinds of home improvements.

Several types of policy issues have become sufficiently commonplace for specific types of impact analyses to have evolved for these areas. The best known of these is probably the environmental impact assessment or statement. These analyses were mandated by the National Environmental Policy Act of 1969 for a wide variety of proposals, ranging from power stations to parking lots. Today, in fact, any undertaking that may have a significant effect on the surrounding environment, which is in any way supported by federal money or subject to federal regulation, must be preceded by an environmental impact analysis.[63]

Environmental impact assessment was originally stimulated by concern for our built and natural environment. Traditional environmental impact statements concerned the effects of policies or projects on air and water quality, plant life, and on animals, birds, and fish. Later, people began to realize that human beings are just as much part of the environment as all these others, so that the effect of technology on people deserves equal concern. This led to social impact assessment, now a standard element in environmental impact statements.[64]

The above are all evaluation approaches that can be used for cases with one inclusive goal, or a set of compatible objectives, and with a single and homogenous organization, institution, or interest group as the client. Many planning issues, however, involve conflicting goals and multiple interests. The parties in conflict will quickly raise the issue of equity if the planning group forgets it. They will be concerned with incidence and distribution as well as—if not more than—the total of costs and benefits. The equity criterion asks of each option, "Who gets hurt?"

There are evaluation methods that have been developed specifically for such planning problems, that attempt to combine assessments of efficiency and equity. One of these is the "Planning Balance Sheet," developed by

Lichfield and his associates as an extension of benefit-cost analysis, to include nonmonetary and distributional considerations.[65] Another is the "Goals-Achievement Matrix" that Hill devised to reflect the impact of alternative proposals on the objectives of different interest groups, objectives which could be given different priorities, as, indeed, could the groups themselves.[66] These more "qualitative" evaluation methods, though less widespread and well known than more "quantitative" methods such as benefit-cost analysis, have been successfully used to select alternative proposals in areas as diverse as urban expansion plans, power station siting, or airport location.[67]

Implementation

Once, descriptions of the planning process would have concluded with the selection of a preferred alternative, and its communication in the form of a plan. Today, as we have seen, we are more conscious of the link between planning and action,[68] and implementation then becomes an indivisible part of the process that links intentions with results.

One result of this change in attitude is that implementation has become the subject of a good deal of attention. A number of approaches to implementation have emerged; one is a "classical" sequential model:

> Implementation is the carrying out of a basic policy decision, usually made in a statute...the implementation process normally runs through a number of stages beginning with passage of the basic statute, followed by the policy outputs (decisions) of the implementing agencies, the compliance of target groups..., the *actual* impacts—both intended and unintended—of these outputs, the *perceived* impacts of agency decisions, and, finally, important revisions (or attempted revisions) in the basic statute.[69]

Others suggest a variety of implementation processes, depending on the circumstances. Such processes may range from "programmed" implementation, like that described above, through "adaptive," "circular," or even "evolutionary" implementation.[70] These views suggest that policies are not just made and implemented, or plans drawn up and executed. Rather, policymaking, planning, program design, and project, program, or plan implementation are interlinked through continuous participant interaction and adaptation between those legislating policy or developing plans and those who modify or adapt policies and plans when carrying them out.[71]

The lack of agreement on how to conceptualize the process of implementation probably accounts for how little we still know about it.[72] Nevertheless, a few generalizations are possible. A strong political commitment appears to be a necessary, but not always sufficient, condition for the adoption and successful realization of proposals. Clearly defined goals, which are translatable into objectives that can be monitored, are important. Last, simple projects that can be executed within a framework of relative organizational autonomy are more likely to succeed than complex plans that require the cooperation of numerous interdependent units.[73]

Finale

The process described here would probably command the consensus of most practicing planners, even if there are disagreements between scholars and observers of the planning process about the degree to which it represents an ideal, rather than describing what really takes place. Do we always diagnose problems and search for solutions, or are answers just as often looking for questions? Can we usually identify goals, or is it easier to plan without goals? Is it possible to develop and evaluate options as required by the process described above, or are decision makers more usually just satisfied with a proposal that meets some minimal requirements?

Alternative approaches to planning and decision-making have been proposed, as we have seen, and there is some evidence that they are better descriptions of the way decision-making actually occurs in many situations. But the planning process as it has been set out here is still the prevailing paradigm. Though planning practice is changing, and recent theories have shown sensitivity to many issues which the "classical" rational planning model fails to address, this model of what should be done has yet to be superseded.

Discussion Questions and Exercises

1. How would you define planning? Remember, your definition should ensure that planning is distinguished from other, nonplanning, activities. After all, planning is not everything, and everything is not planning. Give some examples to illustrate the distinctions you make.

2. Which of the following definitions of planning is *not* correct?

    (a) Planning is forethought;

     (b) Planning is the process of determining future action through a sequence of choices;

     (c) Planning is waht planners do;

     (d) Planning is trial-and-error.

3. Is it true that every objective observer of a situation would arrive at an identical diagnosis of its problem(s)? Explain, and give an example to prove your case.

4. Is it easy to identify the goals of a community or an organization (as distinct from an individual defining his/her own objectives)? What are some of the problems that might make it difficult to define goals? Illustrate with some concrete examples from your reading or experience.

5. Is prediction of future trends and of the possible outcomes of alternative courses of action an essential part of the planning process? Give the reasons for your answer, and illustrate your case with some actual planning situations.

6. You have been given three alternative sites for a proposed solid waste recycling facility for the city where you are employed as a planner, and have been asked to evaluate them. Should you simply proceed with the evaluation? If so, why? If not, why not? What would you do before evaluating the given set of alternative sites if you feel that something prior to evaluation is warranted?

7. Some steps in the planning process are:

     (a) Feasibility analysis;

     (b) Prediction and projection;

     (c) Goal articulation/problem diagnosis;

     (d) Alternatives' design;

     (e) Implementation;

     (f) Evaluation.

What sequence of these stages best describes the rational planning process?

8. Give an example of a comparison between two projects/programs that

you would evaluate using benefit-cost analysis. Explain why this kind of evaluation would be more appropriate than another.

9. You are asked to evaluate several alternative neighborhood revitalization programs that are proposed by different community organizations requesting allocations of Community Development funds. Which of the following evaluation methods might you use, and what are the considerations affecting your choice?

  (a) Benefit-cost analysis;
  (b) Cost-effectiveness analysis;
  (c) Planning balance sheet or goals-achievement analysis;
  (d) Impact analysis (social-environmental-economic, etc.).

10. Research into implementation suggests some factors that make successful implementation more likely; which of the following have been identified as such factors?

  (a) A simple plan/program/project, within the power of one agency to carry out;
  (b) The power, on the part of the agency proposing a policy, to legislate the accomplishment of its objectives;
  (c) Clearly stated goals, objectives, and clearly identified means for implementation;
  (d) Involvement of all concerned organizations, to make sure "all bases are covered";
  (e) Maximum feasible citizen participation.

Notes

1. A slightly different version of this section appeared as "If Planning Isn't everything, Maybe It's Something," *Town Planning Review* 52(2) (April 1981), 135-138.
2. J. W. Dyckman, *Introduction to Readings in the Theory of Planning: The State of Planning Theory in America*, mimeo, 1979. H. C. Hightower, *Towards a Definition of Square One: The ACSP School Review Committee and Procedural Planning Theory*, paper presented at the Western Regional Meeting of the Association of Collegiate Schools of Planning, Port Ludlow, Washington, 18 October 1976, p. 1.
3. G. Chadwick, *A Systems View of Planning* (Oxford: Pergamon, 1971) p. 24.
4. G. A. Miller, E. Galanter, and K. H. Pribram, *Plans and the Structure of Behavior* (New York: Holt, 1960).
5. T. Moore, "Why Allow Planners to Do What they Do? A Justification from

WHAT AND HOW? PLANNING DEFINITIONS AND PROCESS

WHAT AND HOW? PLANNING DEFINITIONS AND PROCESS 59

Economic Theory," *Journal of the American Institute of Planners*, 44(4) (October 1978), pp. 387-388.

6. B. Hudson, "Comparison of Recent Planning Theories: Counterparts and Contradictions," *Journal of the American Planning Association* 45(4) (October 1979):387.

7. R. A. Levine, *Public Planning: Failure and Redirection* (New York: Basic Books, 1972), p. 4.

8. R. Ackoff, *A Concept of Corporate Planning* (New York: Wiley, 1970), p. 1.

9. H. Ozbekhan, "Planning and Human Action," in *Hierarchically Organized Systems in Theory and Practice* (P. A. Weiss, ed.), (New York: Haffner, 1971), p. 169.

10. M. J. Webber, "Operational Models in Urban Planning," *Environment and Planning*, 13(6) (December 1981): 764.

11. P. Davidoff, and T. A. Reiner, "A Choice Theory of Planning," *Journal of the American Institute of Planners*, 28(3) (May 1962): 103-115.

12. J. Friedmann, "Notes on Societal Action," *Journal of the American Institute of Planning* 35(4) (September 1969): 312.

13. H. Rittel and M. Webber, "Dilemmas in a General Theory of Planning," *Policy Sciences*, 4(2) (Summer 1973): 155-169.

14. Sir G. Vickers, *Value Systems and Social Process* (New York: Basic Books, 1968).

15. D. Eversley, *The Planner in Society: The Changing Role of a Profession* (London: Faber, 1973).

16. This question is addressed by A. Faludi in *Planning Theory* (Oxford: Pergamon, 1973), pp. 184-185; and by M. Meyerson in "Building the Middle-Range Bridge for Comprehensive Planning," *Journal of the American Institute of Planning*, 22(2) (Spring 1956): 58-64.

17. H. A. Simon, *The New Science of Management Decision* (New York: Harper, 1960), p. 7.

18. S. S. Fainstein and N. I. Fainstein, "City Planning and Political Values," *Urban Affairs Quarterly*, 6(2) (March 1971): 348.

19. M. Meyerson, "Utopian Tradition and the Shaping of Cities," *Daedalus* 90 (Winter 1961): 182.

20. W. Williams, "Implementation Analysis and Assessment," *Policy Analysis* 1(3) (Summer 1975):531-566. W. Williams and R. F. Elmore (eds.), *Social Program Implementation* (New York: Academic Press, 1976).

21. C. E. Banfield, "Notes on a Conceptual Scheme" in *Politics, Planning and the Public Interest* by M. Meyerson and E. C. Banfield (Glencoe, IL: Free Press, 1955): 303-329; J. K. Friend and W. N. Jessop, *Local Government and Strategic Choice*, (London: Tavistock, 1969); N. Lichfield, P. Kettle and M. Whitbread, *Evaluation in the Planning Process* (Oxford: Pergamon, 1973).

22. R. Mack, *Planning on Uncertainty: Decision Making in Business and Government Administration* (New York: Wiley-Interscience): 135-148.

23. E. Stokey and R. Zeckhauser, *A Primer for Policy Analysis* (New York, Norton, 1978), pp. 5-6.

24. See, for example, H. Mintzberg, D. Raisinghani, and A. Theoret, "The Structure of Unstructured Decisions," *Administrative Science Quarterly* 21 (1976): 246-275.

25. K. A. Archibald, "Three Views of the Expert's Role in Policy-Making: Systems Analysis Incrementalism, and the Clinical Approach," *Policy Sciences* 1 (Spring, 1970): 73-86. A more extended example of different analytical approaches eliciting different solutions is given in G. T. Allison, *Essence of Decision: Explaining the Cuban Missile Crisis* (Boston: Little, Brown, 1971).

26. For an illuminating analysis of this phenomenon, see I. A. Mitroff, *The Subjective Side of Science: A Philosophical Enquiry into the Psychology of the Apollo Moon Scientists*, (New York: Elsevier, 1974).

27. R. L. Warren, "The Sociology of Knowledge and the Problems of the Inner Cities," *Social Science Quarterly* 52 (December 1971): 469-491.

28. E. T. Jennings, Jr. and M. P. Smith, "Human Behavior and Policy Studies," in *Teaching Policy Studies* (W. D. Coplin, ed.) (Lexington, Mass.: D. C. Heath, 1978): 45-60.

29. M. A. Lyles and I. A. Mitroff, "Organizational Problem Formulation: An Empirical Study," *Administrative Science Quarterly* 25(1) (March 1980): 102-119.

30. Cohen, March, and Olson, *op. cit.* W. F. Pounds, "The Process of Problem Finding," *Industrial Management Review*, 11 (1969): 1-19.

31. W. K. Warner and A. E. Havens, "Goal Displacement and the Intangibility of Organizational Goals," *Administrative Science Quarterly* 12 (March 1968): 539-555.

32. For a review of the experience with one method, PPBS, see *Public Administration Review* 33 (March-April 1973): 146-156.

33. See, for example, G. C. Edwards, *Implementing Public Policy* (Washington, D.C.: Quarterly Press, 1980): 26-33, 37-39. J. S. Larson, *Why Government Programs Fail* (New York: Praeger, 1980): 114-116; D. A. Mazmanian and P. A. Sabatier, "The Implementation of Public Policy: A Framework for Analysis," in *Effective Policy Implementation* (D. A. Mazmanian and P. A. Sabatier, eds.), (Lexington, Mass.: D. C. Heath, 1981), pp. 10, 25.

34. C. E. Lindblom, op. cit.

35. H. G. Frederickson, op. cit.

36. M. B. McCaskey, op. cit.

37. E. R. Alexander, "Choice in a Changing World," *Policy Sciences* 3(3) (September 1972): 325-337.

38. Reviews of these techniques and others appear in E. Jantsch, *Technological Forecasting in Perspective* (Paris: Organisation for Economic Co-operation & Development, 1967). S. C. Wheelwright and S. Makridakis, *Forecasting Methods for Management* (2d ed.) (New York: Wiley, 1977).

39. This is condensed from E. R. Alexander, "Design in the Planning Process: Theory, Education and Practice," presented to the ACSP National Conference on Planning Education, November 1981, Washington, D.C. E. R. Alexander, "Design in the Decision Making Process," *Policy Sciences*, 14(3) (September 1982): 279-292.

40. L. B. Archer, "An Overview of the Structure of the Design Process," in *Emerging Methods in Design and Planning* (G. T. Moore, ed.), (Cambridge, Mass.: MIT Press, 1970), pp. 285-307.

41. H. A. Simon, *The Sciences of the Artificial* (Cambridge, Mass.: MIT Press, 1969), p. 55.

42. M. Scott, *American City Planning Since 1890* (Berkeley: University of California Press, 1969).

43. D. E. Wilson, *The National Planning Idea in U.S. Public Policy* (Boulder, Col.: Westview Press, 1980), p. 12.

44. E. C. Enthoven, "Ten Practical Principles for Policy and Program Analysis," in *Benefit Cost and Policy Analysis 1974* (R. Zeckhauser et al., ed.) (Chicago: Aldine, 1975), p. 463.

45. E. P. Alexander, "The Design of Alternatives in Organizational Contexts: A Pilot Study," *Administrative Science Quarterly* 42(3) (September 1979):382-404.

46. C. E. Hausman, *A Discourse on Novelty and Creation* (The Hague: Martinus Nijhoff, 1975).

47. D. G. Marquis, "The Anatomy of Successful Innovations," *Innovation*, 1 (1969): 28-37. W. F. Pounds, "The Process of Problem Finding," *Industrial Management Review* 11 (1969): 1-19. H. A. Simon, *Models of Discovery* (Dordrecht-Holland: D. Reidel, 1977).

48. N. J. Nilsson, *Problem Solving Methods in Artificial Intelligence* (New York: McGraw-Hill, 1971), pp. 53, 72, 87.

49. Som repertoires of design methods are offered in J. C. Jones, *Design Methods: Seeds of Human Futures* (New York: Wiley-Interscience, 1970). G. Broadbent, *Design in Architecture: Architecture and the Human Services* (New York: Wiley, 1973) while these are presented in form and space-shaping applications, some are quite suitable for planning and policy-related applications as well.

50. L. Luckman, "An Approach to the Management of Design," *Operational Research Quarterly* 18(4) (1967).

51. F. Zwicky, *Discovery, Invention, Research Through the Morphological Approach* (New York: MacMillan, 1969).

52. G. Nadler, *Work Systems Design: The IDEALS Concept* (Homewood, Ill.: R. D. Irwin, 1967).

53. R. L. Ackoff, *The Art of Problem solving* (New York: Wiley-Intersceince, 1978).

54. H. Dehlinger and J. P. Protzen, "Some Considerations for the Design of Issue Based Information Systems (IBIS)," *DMG-DRS Journal: Design Research and Methods* 6(2) (April-June 1972): 38-45.

55. Two interesting cases of systematic design of alternative policy solutions are Downs' urban policy options: A. Downs, "Alternative Forms of Future Urban Growth in the U.S.," *Journal of the American Institute of Planning* 36(1) (January 1970): 3-11; and the development of alternative health insurance schemes: J. P. Newhouse, C. F. Phelps, and W. B. Schwartz, "Policy Options and the Impact of National Health Insurance," *New England Journal of Medicine*, 290 (June 13, 1974), 1345-1359.

56. Lichfield, Kettle, and Whitbread, op. cit., pp. 15, 20, 25.

57. An example of the analysis of these factors is provided in A. J. Mumphrey, Jr., J. R. Seley, and J. Wolpert, "A Decision Model for Locating Controversial Facilities," *Journal of the American Institute of Planners* 37 (November 1971); 397-402.

58. When intangibles or items which are difficult to quantify make up a significant

proportion of program or project benefits or costs, this poses a problem which can become insuperable. One way of addressing it is to treat these items as a residual; see J. T. Mao, "Efficiency in Public Urban Renewal Expenditures through Benefit-Cost Analysis," *Journal of the American Institute of Planners* 22(2) (March 1966): 95-107.

59. D. S. Sawicki, M. Matichich, and A. Helling, "The No-Action Alternative: A Tool for Comprehensive Planning and Policy Analysis," *Environmental Impact Assessment Review* 2(2) (1982).

60. E. J. Mishan, *Cost Benefit Analysis* (2d ed.) (London: G. Allen, 1971).

61. R. W. Johnson and J. M. Pierce, "The Economic Evaluation of Policy Impacts: Cost-Benefit and Cost Effectiveness Analysis," in *Methodologies for Analyzing Public Policies* (F. P. Scioli, Jr. and T. J. Cook, eds.) (Lexington, Mass.: Heath, 1975), 132.

62. M. B. Teitz, "Cost-Effectiveness: A Systems Approach to Analysis of Urban Services," *Journal of the American Institute of Planners* 34 (November 1968): 303-311.

63. For more detail, see P. Heffernan and P. Corwin (eds.) *Environmental Impact Assessment* (San Francisco: Freeman, Cooper, 1975).

64. C. P. Woolf, "Social Impact Assessment: The State of the Art," in D. Carson (ed.), *Man Environment Interactions: Evaluations and Applications* (Pt. 1) (Stroudsburg, Pa.: Dowden, Hutchinson & Ross, 1974), 1-44.

65. Lichfield, Kettle, and Whitbread, op. cit., pp. 60-62, 65-97.

66. M. Hill, "A Goals-Achievement Matrix for Evaluating Alternative Plans," *Journal of the American Institute of Planners* 34(1) (January 1968): 19-39; M. Hill, *Planning for Multiple Objectives: An Approach to the Evaluation of Transportation Plans* (Philadelphia: Regional Science Research Institute, 1973).

67. Some cases are presented in N. Lichfield, P. Kettle, and M. Whitbread, op. cit., See also M. Hill and R. Alterman, "Power Plant Site Evaluation: A Case Study," *Journal of Environmental Management* 2 (1974): 179-186. D. Miller, "Project Location Analysis Using the Goals Achievement Method of Evaluation," *Journal of the American Institute of Planners* 46(2) (April 1980): 195-208.

68. See E. R. Alexander, "Implementation: Does a Literature Add up to a Theory," *Journal of the American Institute of Planners* 48(1) (Winter 1981): 132-135. R. Alterman, "Implementation Analysis in Urban and Regional Planning: Toward a Research Agenda," in *Planning Theory: Prospects for the 1980s* (G. McDougall and M. Thomas, eds.) (Oxford: Pergamon, 1982).

69. Mazmanian and Sabatier, op. cit., pp. 5-6.

70. P. Berman, "The Study of Macro- and Micro-Implementation," *Public Policy* 20(2) (Spring 1978). R. F. Elmore, "Organizational Models of Social Program Implementation," *Public Policy* 26(2) (Spring 1978). M. Rein and F. B. Rabinowitz, "Implementation: A Theoretical Perspective," in W. D. Burnham and M. W. Weinberg (eds.), *American Politics and Public Policy* (Cambridge, Mass.: MIT Press, 1978). G. Majone and A. Wildavsky, "Implementation as Evolution," in *Policy Studies Review Annual* (Vol. 2) (H. E. Freeman, eds.) (Beverly Hills, Calif.: Sage, 1978).

71. See, for example, A. Wildavsky and J. Pressman, *Implementation* (Berkeley,

Calif.: University of California Press, 1973); E. Bardach, *The Implementation Game* (Cambridge, Mass.: MIT Press, 1977); B. A. Radin, *Implementation, Change, and the Federal Bureaucracy: School Desegregation Policy in H. E. W. 1964-1968* (New York: Teachers College Press, Columbia University, 1977); and W. Williams, *Government By Agency* (New York: Academic Press) for cases illustrating this process; a theoretical framework is presented in E. R. Alexander, "Policy-Planning-Implementation: The 'Missing Link'," in *New Trends in Urban Planning*, D. Soen (ed.) (Oxford: Pergamon, 1979).

72. E. R. Alexander, "From Idea to Action: Notes for a Contingent Theory of the Policy-Implementation Process," *Administration and Society*, 16(4), (February, 1985): 403-426, pp. 403-411.

73. Pressman and Wildavsky, op. cit.; Mazmanian and Sabatier, op. cit.

CHAPTER 4
Models and Roles

Our exploration has taken us through various approaches to what planning is, and has led us, perhaps, to a definition of planning with which we can come to terms. This definition, however, is only enough to tell us something about planning at a very general level of abstraction. What are the various things planners do, and how do they go about carrying out their tasks?

At the same time, we shall find that calling someone "a planner" when he or she is filling a planning position or doing a job involving planning related functions, is an inadequate description of reality. In fact, planners have to assume different roles to undertake different tasks—even though all these duties involve planning, directly or indirectly—in response to changing contexts. To understand better what planning is about, then, we have to look at planning models and planners' roles.

Planning Models

In the effort to describe the various kinds of activity that can be subsumed under planning, widely differing sets of planning models have been proposed. No one of these is more or less true or accurate than any other; rather, the differences are the result of each observer looking at planning from a somewhat different perspective. Clustering these points of view, we can distinguish three major approaches.

The first is, perhaps, the simplest, and most intuitively obvious. It distinguishes planning models according to the object of concern, and as a result, planning is divided up on *substantive* or sectoral-functional lines. Since this often reflects prevailing institutional divisions—in a sense, the way we have organized society—it is certainly one useful way of distinguishing between different types of planning activity, such as physical, economic, transportation, and health planning and the like.

The second is more conceptual, and looks at planning from an *instrumental* point of view: how types of planning differ in what they want to accomplish and the tools they deploy. In this view, one type of planning might aim at coordinating private and public decisions, and use the persuasive power of the technical expertise and superior data and information that are incorporated in the plan as a means toward this end. A different planning approach may aim at controlling the results of private and market transactions, and use the regulatory powers of government to accomplish the plan's prescribed outcomes.

Finally, different planning models can be identified in historical retrospect and contemporary observation. We could call this approach *contextual*. It relates different types of planning to different sociopolitical contexts and ideologies, asking: Who plans for whom with what ideas in mind; These "ideas" encompass both overt planning rationales and the hidden social and political agenda that are a model's strengths and weaknesses.

Substantive Models

Several reviews of planning divide up the field on substantive, sectoral-functional lines.[1] Not surprisingly, these have a great deal in common, reflecting, as they do, the lines on which our social institutions are organized. The following are some of the main functional areas in this classification of planning models.

Physical planning deals with the land and the built environment. In the broadest sense, it "involves the spatial distribution of goals, objects, functions, and activities."[2] If we further divide physical planning by variations in scale, we may distinguish between urban ("city" or "town and country") planning and regional planning, though more often as the scale of the planning area increases, physical planning becomes more inclusive of social and especially economic considerations.[3]

Under physical planning, too, we can include *urban design*, which addresses the built environment at the interface between planning and architecture. Historically, urban design often covered the formal aspects of entire cities, when a city was conceived as a single consciously designed unit; examples range from classical Alexandria to L'Enfant's plan for Washington, D.C. Urban design interventions in an existing urban fabric were also common, such as Nash's terraces in Bath and London and Hausmann's boulevards in Paris.[4] Today, with the exception of new towns projects, urban design is usually more concerned with the meso- and microscale of the built environment, ranging from the neighborhood to the building complex or urban spaces such as plazas, avenues, and malls. In its implementation tools, which include regulation, zoning, and public development, urban design merges into land-use planning and control.[5]

Another aspect of physical planning is *land-use planning*. Land-use planners are concerned with the patterns of location of people—households, firms, and organizations—and their activities, and may attempt to modify locational trends so that they conform to social and public goals.[6] This is undoubtedly the side of physical planning that is most firmly institutionalized through governmental regulation and control of the development process. Even in the United States, public land-use planning is a well-developed function of local government, while many other areas (including Britain, Western Europe, and Scandinavia) have a hierarchy of land-use and developmental controls ranging from local to national levels.[7]

Transportation, public facilities, and infrastructure planning could also be regarded as subsets of physical planning, like land-use planning or urban design. However, historically they have emerged out of a somewhat different tradition—civil and municipal engineering and public works—and are today still separately institutionalized, in terms of recruitment, organization, and statutory mandates. *Transportation planning* covers a range of geographic levels from the region to the street intersection or the multimodal node, and deals with the various modes of transportation—from air travel to bicycle routes—separately and in combination. Transportation planners deploy, in their sector, much the same generic planning process described above, and, since land-use generates travel demand, and access creates the development potential for land, transportation and land-use planning often proceed in intimate interaction.[8]

Another planning arena deals with *public investments* in facilities, infrastructure, other networks, and services. At the local level, the location of buildings and spaces such as schools, libraries, and parks is the concern of the physical or land-use planner, but specialized utilities such as sewerage and water supply, and major facilities such as power stations are the subject of special planning studies and public policy decisions at the regional, state, or national level. Increasingly, planners are becoming involved in capital programming, the process through which public agencies determine the allocations, timing, and locations of their investments in buildings, plant, and infrastructure.

Housing is another sector in which planners are involved. While architects, developers, and individual households are responsible for the physical structure and form of dwelling uints, planners are concerned with policy that affects the location of different types of housing, and the allocation of resources (in the form of in-kind programs such as public housing and neighborhood renewal, or incentives and subsidy programs) that affect the supply of dwelling units and modify housing demand.[9]

Environmental and Resources Planning emerged as a major arena of planning activity in the 1970s, when the natural environment became a focus for social concern. This became institutionalized in the form of legislation such as the Clean Air & Water Acts and new public agencies and voluntary organizations such as the Environmental Protection Agency and the Sierra Club.

Environmental planning rests on a theoretical foundation of ecological concepts that, indeed, are themselves the substructure of an emerging model of "ecological planning" to which we will return. But, like other types of sectoral planning, environmental planning invokes the same generic process presented above. Natural scientists and experts in areas

---

Environmental and Resources Planning

Source: D. A. Wallace and W. C. McDonnell, "Diary of a Plan," Journal of the American Inst. of Planners, 37,1 (Jan. 1971) pp. 15,16. Copyright permission the JAIP, now the JAPA, does not have any note re copyright limitations on its material. The original source for these illustrations is a report, "The Plan for the Valleys," prepared for the Green Spring and Worthington Valley Planning Council Inc. in 1963-4 which is unlikely to have been copyrighted. If copyright permission is sought from the JAPA, the address is: Raymond Burby III and Edward Kaiser, Editors, Center for Urban & Regional Studies, University of North Carolina, Hickerson Hse 067 A, Chapel Hill, NC 27514.

FORESTED PROMONTORIES HIGH RISE LOCATIONS

UNFORESTED VALLEY WALLS NO DEVELOPMENT

FORESTED VALLEY WALLS 1 HOUSE / 3 ACRES

FORESTED PLATEAU 1 HOUSE / 1 ACRE

VILLAGES & HAMLETS

UNFORESTED PLATEAU MIXED DENSITY

COUNTRY TOWN

Forested Valley Walls Development

such as geology, limnology, and botany are drawn upon for the inventory phase, which identifies constraints and resources, and for assistance in projecting the consequences of alternative interventions, but the planner's task is to develop and implement the framework for aggregating these considerations into proposals for public policy.[10]

As a blanket term, environmental planning covers a wide range of concerns, which are addressed in separate organizational contexts and legal mandates. Land-use considerations include identifying environmentally unique or critical areas such as nature preserves, floodplains, and wetlands, and locating potentially environmentally destructive facilities such as nuclear generators, waste disposal areas, and power transmission lines. A resource that has become an important area of planning interest since 1973 is energy. Other environment resources include forests, agricultural land, and the oceans—all of these are subjects of planning and public policy today. Environmental aspects include air pollution, water pollution abatement planning, and solid and hazardous waste disposal. As a device for integrating environmental with other planning considerations, the environmental impact statement (EIS) has become mandatory in many situations.[11]

Social and economic planning cover a number of levels and functional areas. National economic planning is usually left to the economists, but planners are active in *regional and state economic development,*[12] and in *community and neighborhood development planning.*[13] Planners are also moving into decision-related fields such as *budgeting and fiscal management*[14] and *policy analysis,*[15] as the relation of these activities to the generic planning process becomes obvious, and as the usefulness of planning skills is recognized.

As a planning model, we will discuss social planning below, but it is also generally understood to cover functional sectors such as *health, human services, public safety,* and *criminal justice.*[16] As public interest in these areas has waxed and waned, agencies and organizations emerged in these sectors—such as the regional comprehensive health planning agencies, the National Law Enforcement Assistance Administration (LEAA), and local human services coordinating agencies of various kinds—which became the locus of social planning efforts.[17]

Reprise This review of planning activities by functional sectors begs the question that other classifications avoid. Is the extension of the generic label "planning" to such a wide spectrum of activities, each involving its own area of substantive knowledge and specialization, useful or, indeed, meaningful? Are the commonalities that link all these planners greater than their differences? Does a comprehensive land-use planner, for example, have more in common with a development administrator, than he has with a transportation planner, or does a planner in a regional health planning agency have more to talk about with a hospital administrator than she can find to discuss with her planning colleagues in the local housing authority?

The answer to this question is not obvious, and people have legitimately taken opposing positions. While discussion—probably endless—can ensue on the relevance of various theoretical considerations, a pragmatic approach may offer more promising criteria. Such an approach is likely to lead to different conclusions in different national and cultural contexts, which vary in the degree to which and the ways in which planning is institutionalized. Where you stand on this question, then, may depend (like for so many other issues) on where you sit, and American, British, French, or Swedish observers may come to different conclusions, all valid for their respective environments.[18]

Instrumental Models

Unlike the above approach, the instrumental classification of planning models avoids the question of the substantive content of different types of planning activity. Instead, it focuses on the variations in planning objectives and the tools employed to achieve them. Of the classifications presented here it is the most abstract, unrelated as it is to institutional contexts or historical experience. Nevertheless, concrete examples of all the planning types identified here can also be found, and this "conceptual scheme" can be valuable in analyzing real-life planning behavior.[19]

Regulatory planning is probably the kind of planning with which people are most familiar. It describes a desired end-state and regulates private decisions and actions to bring that state about, usually by prohibiting those that are not within approved categories or limits. The classic case of this type of planning is the local master plan and zoning regulations. Naturally, regulatory planning requires the power on the part of the body undertaking the planning process and implementing the plan—a government or a public agency—to legislate and enforce the rules that make the plan's implementation possible. To be effective, this power must extend over the entire area included under the plan, and all the relevant actors in the process of developing this area must be subject to the regulations. Finally, there must be the commitment actually to enforce the

plan's provisions in accordance with its original intent and the social
goals—explicit or implied—that provide the motivation for planning in
the first place.

More often than not, these conditions are not met, and regulatory planning fails. The complexity of urban and metropolitan systems and interactions makes it almost inevitable that the limits of the regulating agency's
control are too narrow to be effective. Too small, fragmented, and over-
lapping jurisdictions, organizations, and institutions which are either
exempt from the regulations, or which are so powerful as to be immune to
sanctions, are some of the reasons for this failure. Another is the lack of
sufficient political commitment, often, to maintain and enforce the plan's
provisions in the face of counterpressure from affected individuals and
interest groups.[20]

The arena in which regulatory planning most readily comes to mind is
physical and land-use planning and development control. While those who
are affected by it tend to notice its impacts at the local level, often local
land-use planning and control are just the bottom level of a multilayered
planning system, ranging up through the county or district, then the region, state, or province, right up to the national level. In this way, national
policy on issues such as urbanization and settlement patterns, industrial
location and economic development, and population relocation or disper-
sal, is implemented—for better or for worse.[21]

Finally, regulatory planning is not confined to land use. Environmental
regulations are an example of regulatory planning deployed to achieve the
social goals of clean air and water and the conservation of our natural
heritage. Economic objectives may be pursued through regulatory planning, which may control the location of industry or regulate the interactions between firms and their employees, competitors, clients, or consumers. Though it may not seem obvious at first blush, the British Board
of Trade, when it assigns construction permits to industrial plants, the
National Labor Relations Board, when it sets rules for labor-management
interaction, or the Consumer Protection Agency when it develops fire
resistance codes for childrens' pajamas, are all engaged in regulatory
planning.

Allocative planning uses different tools to achieve social goals. Where
regulatory planning depends on the power to prohibit the undesirable,
allocative planning depends on the power to provide resources for desirable objectives or activities. The resources allocated may be the agency's
own: budgeting is this type of allocative planning, where a government,

institution, or organization determines for what purposes its funds or expected revenues will be spent.

On the other hand, the resources allocated may be others'. Tax incentives may be used, for example, to reallocate industrial investment to peripheral regions or areas with high unemployment; this has been done in many countries, including Britain, France, Italy, Israel, the United States, and many more.[22] Responsibilities, sometimes perceived as burdens, may be allocated too. Under the U.S. Department of Housing and Urban Development's "Fair Share" housing policy, for example, regional and local planners determine what proportion of an area's low-income housing needs each community must meet if it is to be eligible for federal funds.[23]

As these examples suggest, often one type of planning blends into—or uses the tools of—another. Here allocative planning actually becomes an instrument to implement developmental purposes, as in the first example, or itself uses regulative tools, as in the second.

Development planning is often used to refer to planning in and for less developed nations.[24] In this sense, planning is primarily seen as a way of promoting the economic and social advancement of these countries. Planning for less developed countries, or LDCs as they are now called, emerged as a distinct area of activity after World War II, and since then it has gone through several phases, mainly as a result of disillusionment with the results of each previous approach, and related changes in economic doctrine.[25] So the "big push" doctrine or massive capital-intensive development on all fronts, associated with complex economic planning models at the national level, was succeeded by attempts at "unbalanced development," associated with concentration of investments and planning efforts on "growth poles." **Rural and agricultural development** planning, ranging from the high- to medium-technology ideas that created the "green revolution" in some Asian countries to "grass-roots" cooperatives tried in Africa, also had its phases and fads. Today development planning is probably more pragmatic than before, and has abandoned attempts at high-level coordination to focus on project development, evaluation, and implementation at the local and regional levels.[26]

Indicative planning is probably the kind of planning with which non-planners are least familiar, but it is perhaps the kind of planning that is the most common. Each of the kinds of planning discussed above depends on a different kind of power: the power to regulate actions (regulative planning), or the power to allocate resources (allocative and development planning). Indicative planning depends on the power of persuasion: the persuasion of solid information and analysis, of well-based projections of trends and prediction of future conditions, of appealing future scenarios and alternative strategies, and of evaluation criteria with which the people who review the plan, and who are called upon to adopt its proposals, can identify.

Indicative plans, then, rely on the power of persuasion to affect the decisions of firms, organizations, and households. Usually they also indicate the plans and decisions of the public unit itself, which is preparing the plan. To the extent that this unit is powerful, controls resources, and can regulate the actions of others, and is perceived as being committed to its own plan, the plan will also affect the decisions of others. Finally, others' actions may also be influenced by the plan, to the extent that they participated in its preparation and identify with its goals and targets. Accordingly, interaction with the major affected parties and their active involvement in the planning process is an important prerequisite for indicative planning to be implemented.[27]

Traditional comprehensive or master planning at the local level, where it transcends the limits of what local government can regulate through zoning and land-use control, is indicative planning. The participation of important interests such as the Chamber of Commerce, local financial institutions and developers, organized labor, neighborhood organizations, voluntary groups representing specific ideologies and concerns (like the Sierra Club and the League of Women Voters), and citizens at large, may be critical for the plan's acceptance and success. At a higher level, another example of indicative planning is the French five-year national economic plan—*Le Plan*—prepared by a special agency in the French Finance Ministry, the Commisariat du Plan. This effort was given credit—some of it undeserved, perhaps—for France's economic performance in the late 1960s.[28] Its general acceptance and acknowledged usefulness, at least, as a common framework for public and private investment decisions, was as much due to the broad range of participants in the planning process as to the French government's deep involvement in the national economy and the intimate linkage between the public and private sectors.

Reprise Even the few concrete examples cited above show clearly that none of these planning types exist in real life in pure form. Real planning is always a mixture of several of these planning approaches. This typology is useful, however, in analyzing planning behavior and as a conceptual framework for the conscious practitioner. The planner who realizes, for example, that the comprehensive planning process in which he is involved is a mixture of regulative, developmental and indicative planning will do a better job. He will be more aware of the limits of regulation, more conscious of the developmental potential that the plan may unlock, and more attuned to the need to involve those parties that are to be persuaded by the indicative parts of the plan.

Contextual Models

In looking at the historical emergence of planning as a distinct area of activity, we can identify a succession of another kind of planning models. These relate more to their context in time, social institutions, and value-ideological premises than they do either to the substantive object of planning or to the tools deployed to effect the plan's objectives. Some of these are presented below.

Comprehensive Planning

The comprehensive planning model evolved from the physical planning model that prevailed in the 1920s and the 1930s. It recognizes the complexity of factors affecting and affected by what were previously perceived as purely physical or land-use decisions. These factors include social and demographic characteristics of population; economic variables, such as income and local or regional economic base; and transportation factors, travel patterns, modal split, and transportation networks. Comprehensive planning aims to take all these factors into account in a rational, analytic planning process.[29]

During the 1950s and into the early 1960s this model was the dominant one in planning practice. It is still widely applied in land-use planning by local government. Comprehensive planning was institutionalized in the 701 program of the Housing Act of 1954 (which required local governments to prepare comprehensive plans to be eligible for federal grants and programs).

The comprehensive planning model is based on a technocratic ideology that accepts the scientific legitimacy of the planner's expertise. It assumes that the planner knows or can discover other people's needs, and that a central planning agency has the authority and autonomy to develop planning proposals through rational analysis, as well as the power to implement them.[30] Comprehensive planning has been criticized for these assumptions, and for what some have seen as its acceptance of the status quo, support of the political establishment, and perpetuation of middle-class values.[31]

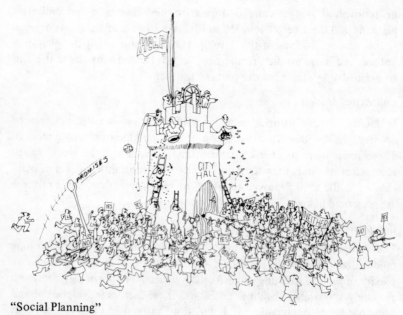

"Social Planning"

Source: Hedman, *op. cit.*, p. 30; copyright: permission (and plates) from Richard Hedman, San Francisco, CA.

Social Planning

Social planning evolved in the 1960s, when comprehensive planning concepts were brought into the arena of social and human services. It allows for consideration of the wants of particular groups and involves the extensive use of social science techniques for identification of these needs. This planning approach is oriented to social needs more than to the physical environment. In contrast to the environmental determinism of earlier design-based planning—that is, its assumption that human behavior can be changed by the physical environment—social planning aims to intervene directly in social interactions. Social planning has had its greatest impact on the planning of goverment-supported programs, such as those dealing with welfare, health, education, and labor.[32]

Social planning has certain ideological shortcomings. Its assumptions of a central authority and benevolent therapist-planners raise questions about legitimacy and participation in decision making.[33] While its political implications are democratic, and less authoritarian than the comprehensive approach, its client orientation is a concession to the multiplicity of conflicting interests in a plural society.

Advocacy Planning

Reacting to the centralist and technocratic values of the prevailing planning modes in the mid-1960s, some planners created a model of planning that was analogous to the U.S. legal system, which they called advocacy planning. The role proposed for planners was to be similar to that of lawyers in the adversary legal system. Advocacy planning was based on the realization that society is not homogeneous but consists of many groups with different interests and values. In this plural society, power is unequally distributed, and access to resources is not the same for the rich and the poor or the educated and the ignorant.[34]

The advocate planner would be a spokesperson for the poor, neighborhoods, or other groups with inadequate access to government. He or she would provide them with the expertise they need to make their voices heard in public decision making. This role was institutionalized in many of the War on Poverty programs of the 1960s, such as the Community Action and Model Cities programs. It continues to be played out today in some community planning efforts and consumer and environmental activism.[35]

Although it corrected some of the biases of other planning models, advocacy planning has limitations. The appropriateness of its legal model in the political context is questionable. Where there is no law, no judge, and no jury, the distribution of power will resolve conflicting interests through political arbitration. The advocate planner's best case may not be good enough in that arbitration if compromise does not occur. Some doubt that advocacy planning can go as far as necessary in correcting the unequal distribution of resources.[36] Finally, some question whether any planner can really represent the poor or other excluded groups. Once such a group is identified as a client, it develops its own spokespersons who become its liaison with the planners.[37]

Bureaucratic Planning

Under bureaucratic planning, the planner is the servant of government and its elected officials. The planner takes on the role of a value-neutral administrator.[38] Since bureaucratic planning is more role- than process-oriented, it is not associated with any one style, although it appears often in planning descriptions of more centralized countries such as Great Britain and France.[39] An emphasis on rationality and systematic analysis leads to the comprehensive planning approach. On the other hand, the bureaucrat planner focusing on feasibility and implementation in a pluralistic environment like American local government may adopt the incremental model described below.

Radical or Anti-Planning

The late 1960s and early 1970s have also seen a number of proposals for the involvement of planners in social change outside the governmental establishment or in active opposition to it. These schemes range from ideological reorientation through community self-regulation and self-help to communitarian planning philosophies.[40]

The trouble with these proposals, as some of their initiators have recognized, is that they can never be more than interstitial in society as we know it. The radical planners, once they have won the battle against the status quo, cannot avoid becoming part of the very institutions they have sworn to alter. Furthermore, many of these models depend on the trust and intimacy of small-group interactions, which have to be replaced by the hierarchy, rules, and accountability of a formal organization when the group's activities grow.

Nonplanning

Several versions of what we call nonplanning have been proposed. They are all based on laissez-faire premises; that is, that people's behavior and interactions will eventually produce socially optimal outcomes with a minimum of regulation.

The incremental decision model, which was developed in reaction to the limitations of rational analysis, is an example of such an approach. It suggests that policies should be developed by trial and error instead of deliberate planning.[41] The value of the model is illustrated by the unregulated but orderly growth of Houston, Texas, and by a proposal for the experimental deregulation of southeastern England.[42]

Ultimately, the ideal mix between planning and nonplanning is a product of the planner's ideology, view of society, and values. To the extent that one agrees with the moderates that the status quo is good and needs only minor changes, with the anarchists that human nature is intrinsically good and is only perverted by rules and controls, or with the cynics that it will do more harm than good to attempt to stretch the narrow limits of our perfectibility, rationality, and ability to control our own futures, one will accept nonplanning to some degree. But if one believes that change is both necessary and possible, and that the outcome of many individually sensible decisions is often a state of affairs nobody wants, or that some beneficial control of our own futures is possible, then one will be more sensitive to the limits of the nonplanning approach.

Reprise Like geological strata in a landscape, these models of planning persist in different contexts, sometimes even side by side. A county's planning department may be engaged in comprehensive planning, while at the same time its housing authority, in developing a program to provide housing for the elderly, is actually in a social planning mode. The same meeting, where representatives of city agencies, neighborhood organizations, and perhaps the planning department's community planner are all participating, involves comprehensive planning, advocacy planning, and perhaps counterplanning all in simultaneous interaction.

Unlike previous periods since the emergence of the comprehensive planning model, our time is one of doubt and uncertainty. We have seen that, until recently, each period was characterized by a dominant mode of planning, in theory if not in practice: Always one type of planning was "in" or the "coming thing." That is hardly true today, and none of the proponents of any of the models presented above would claim that their approach is the wave of the future. The only hint of an exception is an occasional proposal for "ecological planning": planning based on a recognition of the mutual interdependence of natural, human, and societal systems, and employing ecological concepts and tools.[43] However, the proponents of this approach display none of the messianic zeal that characterized the missionaries of comprehensive planning in the 1940s and 1950s, of social planning in the 1960s, or of advocacy planning or radical planning in the late 1960s and early 1970s. As of this writing, "ecological planning" does not seem to be catching on as a popular concept either among planning theorists or practitioners, nor does anyone seem to see it as a wave of the future.

What, then, is the wave of the future in planning? The dominant mood today is probably best characterized as skepticism: a consciousness of the limits of planning and a new concern with the realities of practice and the "nuts-and-bolts" of implementation. This is reflected, on the one hand, in some theorists' interest in the interactive aspects of day-to-day planning practice, and, on the other, in attempts to understand implementation and its successes and failures. Whether, out of these current concerns a new model of planning—perhaps more pragmatic, realistic, and action-orient than its predecessors—will emerge, only time will tell.

Meanwhile, how are intelligent planners to find their way among all these ideas on how the planning process does or could take place? What use can this welter of competing concepts be to them in their day-to-day practice? In part, the answer to these questions has to take us back to the beginning of this book: theory provides a framework of concepts that help one to understand an otherwise baffling environment. But which of the many models of planning reviewed here is realistic or appropriate in a given situation?

Obviously, the context in which a planner is working will limit the range of applicable models: a strategic planner in a metropolitan transportation authority or a facilities planner for the local sewerage district are unlikely to consider "radical planning," for example, without also thinking of changing their jobs. On the other hand, the neighborhood planner with the city planning commission, and the community planner with the neighborhood coop, may both find models from social planning, through advocacy, to "incrementalism" worth considering.

The adoption of a particular model in a given situation, or the development of one's own blend of practice, can only be a matter of judgment, and no formula has yet been devised that will link one approach with a specific context with any assurance of success. What the repertoire of models reviewed above does provide is a vocabulary of concepts to stretch planners' awareness of who they are and what they are doing, and give them the tools for a critical consciousness of the relationship between their personal and professional goals, their planning activity, and the organizational and social environment in which they enact their planning roles.

Planners' Roles

As the planning profession evolved, and with the proliferation of planning activities, planners' roles have grown increasingly diverse. Several studies have concluded that some roles are more effective in certain contexts than others; this reinforces what we would expect based on experience and common sense. Some of the roles that planners may fill are described be-

inistrator

~le of the planner in governmental contexts: the ~rvice of elected officials. The role can be effec-
~rs delegate authority to planners. The planner can

apply professional expertise to effect objectives that have been well-defined by the policymakers with confidence that government can muster the support and resources necessary for their realization.

Frequently, however, this situation is the ideal rather than the reality, and the expected relationship between administrative planner and politician breaks down or never even develops. This may happen when the government represents a diversity of interests that are rarely reconciled in the consensus necessary for effective action. Then the neutral administrator role must be supplemented or superseded by one of the other roles before the planner's proposals can have an impact on policy.[44]

Mobilizer

Often the planner must actively develop support for plan implementation. She may assume the role of a mobilizer, making allies of government agencies or appealing to the public at large, directly or through the media. Since these actions can put the planner at odds with elected officials who are against the policies he or she advocates, the planner is assuming a political role. Political roles put the planner at risk. If he fails, or even does not succeed in mobilizing enough of a constituency in his support, the planner may find himself out of a job. However, in some contexts the planning function in itself may involve a mobilizing role, where planners have to develop a constituency to legitimize their efforts; some cases of neighborhood planning have displayed this effect.[45]

Mediator

Another political role which the planner may have to assume so as to get the planning process under way or to enable implementation of the plan's proposals is that of the mediator, or broker. Here the planner's technical expertise has to be joined with political instincts and interactive skills to combine diverse and sometimes conflicting interests into a supportive coalition. The planner's particular contribution may be in identifying problems of common concern, in developing proposals that can address these problems and at the same time bridge differences between parties or give each of the involved interests something they want. Thus, the planning process may become instrumental in developing consensus among a previously fragmented constituency around a set of mutually agreeable proposals.

Entrepreneur

Another role, less overtly public but political nonetheless, is that of entrepreneur. The entrepreneur wins support for plans by gathering the resources needed to carry them out. In this role, the planner puts together the funds, as well as the necessary administrative approval and political support, to implement plans. The planner often develops entrepreneurial proposals specifically to generate resources for the organization. The success of such efforts gives the entrepreneur planner the necessary base for implementing other plans, which may have fewer obvious and short-term benefits.

Advocate and Guerrilla

The advocate role means the representation of special interest groups. These range from neighborhood residents to poor people to organizations, such as churches, consumer agencies, or corporations.

As discussed earlier, the citizen participation required by federal programs in the 1960s meant that the role of the advocate planner became institutionalized. Though most of these programs no longer exist, the advocate planning role lives on in issue-oriented groups such as the Suburban Action Institute, the Sierra Club, and consumer organizations.

The development of neighborhood planning programs has led to the institutionalization of the advocate role in city government. The neighborhood planners, although employed and paid by city hall, are expected to be advocates for the special interests of their communities, sometimes in opposition to the more general public interest represented by the city planning agency.

The advocate role does bring planning a step closer to the people, but often results in an ambivalent situation. Sometimes it creates community planners who are "guerrillas" in the bureaucracy, and the role conflicts have not yet been satisfactorily resolved.[46]

Other Roles

The roles presented above are limited to particular contexts, or have to be assumed under particular conditions to succeed. A planner working for a strong chief executive in a well-organized city may well be most effective in a technical-administrative role. Trying to act as a broker may be unnecessary, and if she does succeed in putting together a coalition it may be perceived as an attempt to grab power, and she may lose her job. On the other hand, a planner working for a poor neighborhood may have to be a mobilizer first, then a mediator, and at the same time become an entrepreneur to attract outside resources into the community. Limiting his efforts to technical-administrative assistance and advice may doom the planner here to impotence.

Some observers have suggested other roles for planners. What these have in common, in contrast to the roles we have discussed, is their inclusive character, often in reaction to the traditional technical-professional role prescribed for the planner. For example, William Baer has suggested that planners might regard themselves as *midwives*, rather than the prevailing image of the expert, more analogous to the physician. In other words, the planner is assisting a process of decision making and policy development in which, while he is not the main actor, he is an important facilitator.[47]

Another effort to demystify the planner's expertise presents the planner as *adviser*. In this view:

> Advice and planning are human activities that make sense of the world by talking about it. . .When we give advice, we tell stories, and when we plan we are figuring out what to do with others. So advice and planning naturally go together.[48]

While intuitively attractive, the idea of planning as advice fails to come to grips with the question of why the planner should be qualified to give advice. It ends up straddling the range from empathy—the neighbor who understands your problems because he shares them—to the "transcedent claim" for sacred knowledge: the planner as buddy to the planner as priest.

Nevertheless, the idea of the planner as advisor generates some useful insights. For example: "How advisors are wrong depends on the kind of claims they make to being right."[49] This suggests that much of the shadow that has fallen on planning in the last decade may be directly due to the inflated claims made previously. The advisor's role for the planner envisages an interaction between planner and client where the planner's claim of expertise has to be mutually agreed upon and accepted, a claim that can only be commensurate with his capabilities for performance.

Finally, some have come to see planners as *interpreters* or *communicators*. This approach suggests that how planners develop and present proposals is perhaps even more important than the content of the proposals themselves. The planner here is a mediator in a process of social interaction, and the quality of her transmission may critically affect outcomes.

This idea is the result of two streams of thought. One is the phenomenological view of the world—that is, that peoples' actions are the result of how they perceive and experience events around them, rather than of any objective reality, if, indeed, any such reality could be agreed upon by everyone.[50]

The second is a school of thought that sees social and political interactions as encompassing what are traditionally regarded as "objective" science and knowledge.[51] Consequently, the mediators of such knowledge, or experts, have to be conscious of their roles, and of the organizational, class, or cultural biases and interests of the messages they create and transmit.[52]

The planner's role as interpreter and communicator is to present to society—in the form of decision makers and affected constituencies in governments, institutions, and organizations—a version of reality and of the interventions possible to change it. The planning process, then, is an ongoing dialogue among the participating public, with the active mediation of the planners, to arrive at a societal consensus on what is happening, and what can be done to change what is amiss.

What do these views imply for how planners should act in practice? This question is only beginning to be explored, and the answers as yet offer no earth-shattering insights. However, all the implications suggest a much more responsive, interactive, and experience-based mode of planning, and less reliance on analysis by scientific methods, or on a rational planning method that aims to persuade by the reasonableness of its proposals and the objectivity of its information.[53]

Reprise As with planning models, planners' roles have come to display an amazing diversity, both in theory and in practice. The planner can be anything: from a back-room technician (perhaps a "grey-eminence" in the evolution of policy) analyzing the implications of the output of a computerized land-use model, to an advocate presenting a community's "counter plan" to the local council; from an entrepreneur hobnobbing in the corridors-of-power with the officials of national funding agencies, of banks and insurance corporations, or of benevolent foundations, to an administrator-bureaucrat amending the wording of a zoning ordinance; from a communicator at the same time understanding the problems of a neighborhood group and winning their trust, to an advisor telling a community and its elected officials the story of what their city might become, and how to make it happen.

Today, the only thing that is certain about planners' roles is uncertainty: the changeability of roles in different contexts, the ambiguity of previously unquestioned claims of scientific infallibility and professional expertise, and the continuing emergence of novel views of planners' roles with the diffusion of different views of human and societal relations. As a result, the burden on the individual planner is heavier than it has ever been before. Expectations are as high as ever, but no one—not the theorists, not the educators, nor even experienced and successful practitioners—has any norms of role behavior to suggest beyond the kind of truisms that are easily accessible to common sense: adapt your role to your situation, become worthy of the trust of the people you work with, and so on. In the next chapter, we shall explore the implications of this uncertainty for the way planners view themselves, and the way planning is viewed by society.

Discussion Questions and Exercises

1. In your community, region, or State, think of an example of each of the following substantive planning areas:

   (a) Land-use planning;
   (b) Urban design;
   (c) Transportation planning;
   (d) Planning public investments in facilities and infrastructure;
   (e) Housing;
   (f) Environmental planning;
   (g) Energy planning;
   (h) Regional/state economic development;
   (i) Neighborhood and community development;
   (j) Health planning.

   In each case, identify who (institutions and roles) does it, who the clients are, what the results and effects (if any) have been.

2. In the case described above, identify the kinds of instrumental planning models deployed: regulatory planning, allocative planning, developmental planning, or indicative planning. How did these models succeed in their aims, and if they did not, try to identify the reasons for the failure.

3. Which of the following assumptions characterizes comprehensive planning, and which does not?

   (a) There is a common public interest that can be identified by planners;
   (b) Rational analysis can diagnose problems and develop strategies to address them;
   (c) Each community is made up of different groups and interests, each

with equally legitimate goals and values, and conflicts between them can only be resolved by the political process;

(d) Planners can deploy their scientific expertise to identify public goals and objectives, analyze situations and diagnose problems, and propose appropriate respones;

(e) A central general-government agency is empowered to implement the plan's proposals.

4. Describe an application of comprehensive planning that you know about: What was the responsible agency? What area or jurisdiction did the planning effort cover? What was the planning process? How were the plan's proposals articulated? Was the plan adopted, and if so, by whom? If it was not adopted, why not? If it was adopted, have its proposals been implemented, and how? What have been the effects, if any, of the comprehensive planning process described?

5. Which of the following describe the primary focus of social planning:

(a) Human services program delivery;

(b) Optimal development of the physical urban environment;

(c) Representation of the poor in city government;

(d) Addressing the needs of selected client groups.

6. Describe an application of social planning that you know about: Who was the responsible agency? What was the problem addressed, and who were the relevant clients? What programs, if any, were developed and deployed to address the problem, and what were their effects?

7. The model for advocacy planning was taken from which of the following:

(a) The Scandinavian ombudsman system;

(b) The adversary system in legal practice;

(c) The U.S. Constitution;

(d) The Magna Carta;

(e) The legal concept of torts.

8. Advocacy planning is supposed to address which of the following problems:

(a) The poor's lack of education and of access to information sources;

(b) Unequal distribution of professional expertise between the "establishment" and less privileged socioeconomic classes;
(c) Apathy and alienation in society;
(d) The creeping dominance of "secular humanism."

9. Identify and describe a case of nonplanning or of incremental decision making. Why does it fit this classification?

10. Which combination of the following roles would you adopt to maximize your chances of success, in each of the following cases, and why?

(a) technician;
(b) bureaucrat-administrator;
(c) mobilizer;
(d) mediator;
(e) entrepreneur.

A. You are a planner for an inner-city neighborhood that is poor, has many minority residents or is broken up into several different ethnic groups, and is generally fragmented and unorganized.
B. You are a planner working for a well-organized, working-class neighborhood organization that aims to provide services to its members and to affect city government's decisions regarding the area.
C. You are planning director for a small town with several informal power brokers in the community; the mayor and council are weak, and there is no clear developmental program.
D. You are the planning director for a medium-sized city with a strong mayor, clear political consensus, and well-articulated developmental aims.

Notes

1. See, for example, Burchell and Sternlieb (1978), op. cit., and A. J. Catanese and J. S. Snyder (eds.), *Introduction to Urban Planning*, (New York: McGraw-Hill, 1979), 175-341.
2. L. Witzling, "Physical Planning," pp. 175-205 in Catanese and Snyder (eds.), op. cit.; Burchell and Sternlieb (eds.), op. cit., pp. xix-xxvii.
3. The literature on regional planning is extensive; see, for example, J. Friedmann and W. Alonso, *Regional Policy: Readings in Theory and Applications* (Cambridge, Mass.: MIT Press, 1975); J. Alden and R. Morgan, *Regional Planning: A Comprehensive View* (New York: Wiley, 1974); and W. Isard, *Introduction to Regional Science* (Englewood Cliffs, N.J.: Prentice Hall, 1975).

4. See A. F. J. Morris, *History of Urban Form: Prehistory to the Renaissance* (New York: Halstead Press, 1974); E. Y. Galantay, *New Towns: Antiquity to the Present* (New York: Braziller, 1975).
5. R. M. Beckley, "Urban Design," in Catanese and Snyder (eds.) op. cit.; E. N. Bacon, Design of Cities (New York: Penguin, 1974); J. Barnett *Urban Design as Public Policy* (New York: Architectural Record, 1974).
6. W. P. Farmer, and J. A. Gibb, "Land Use Planning," pp. 234-258 in Catanese and Snyder (eds.) op cit.; C. M. Haar, *Land Use Planning: A Case Book on the Use, Misuse, and Reuse of Urban Land* (Boston: Little-Brown, 1971); L. B. Burrow, *Growth Management: Issues, Techniques and Policy Implications* (New Brunswick, N.J.: Center for Urban Policy Research-Rutgers University, 1973).
7. See A. L. Strong, *Planned Urban Environments: Sweden, Finland, Israel, The Netherlands, France* (Baltimore: Johns Hopkins University Press, 1971); for Britain, see P. McAuslan, *Land, Law and Planning* (London: Weidenfeld & Nicholson, 1975); and J. B. Cullingsworth, *Town and Country Planning in Britain* (6th ed.) (London: Allen & Unwin, 1976); for Britain and Western Europe, see N. Lichfield and H. Darin-Drabkin, *Land Policy in Planning* (London: Allen & Unwin, 1980).
8. E. Beimborn, "Transportation and Public Facilities Planning," pp. 259-279 in Catanese and Snyder (eds.) op. cit.; R. L. Creighton, *Urban Transportation Planning* (Urbana, Ill.: Illinois Press, 1970); P. W. Daniels, and A. M. Warnes, *Movement in Cities: Spatial Perspectives on Urban Transportation and Travel* (New York: Methuen, 1980).
9. S. B. White, "Housing," pp. 280-296 in Catanese and Snyder (eds.) op. cit.; R. Montgomery and D. R. Mandelker (eds.), *Housing in America* (2nd ed.), (New York: Bobbs-Merrill, 1979); J. Pynoos, R. Shafer, and C. W. Hartman (eds.), *Housing Urban America* (2nd ed.) (Hawthorne, N.J.: Aldine, 1980).
10. D. C. Hoeh, "Environmental Planning," pp. 206-233 in Catanese and Snyder (eds.) op. cit.; J. McEvoy, III, and T. Dietz (eds.), *Handbook for Environmental Planning: The Social Consequences of Environmental Change*, (New York: Wiley, 1977).
11. See C. A. Coop, "Legal Requirements for Environmental Impact Reporting," pp. 11-64 in McEvoy and Dietz (eds.) op. cit.; and R. F. Munn, (ed.) *Environmental Impact Assessment Principles and Procedures* (2nd ed.), (New York: Wiley, 1979).
12. See, for example, A. Downs, *Neighborhoods and Urban Development* (Washington, D.C.: Brookings Institution, 1981); J. M. Levy, *Economic Development Programs for Cities, Counties and Towns* (New York: Praeger, 1981); D. Marino, *The Planner's Role in Facilitating Private Sector Reinvestment* (Chicago: American Planning Association, 1979).
13. E. R. Alexander and S. C. Kaeser, "Contexts and Roles in Neighborhood Planning: Five Wisconsin Neighborhoods," Proceedings of the APA National Planning Conference, Dallas, Texas, May 1981, presents the role of planning in neighborhood development in a positive light; the opposite view is presented in R. Cohen, "Neighborhood Planning and Political Capacity," *Urban Affairs*

MODELS AND ROLES 89

Quarterly 14(3) (March 1979): 337-362; a lively presentation of the neighborhood planning process is R. Cassidy, *Livable Cities: A Grass-Roots Guide to Rebuilding Urban America* (New York: Holt, Rinehart, and Winston, 1980).

14. See, for example, J. C. Snyder, *Fiscal Management and Planning in Local Government* (Lexington, Mass.: D. C. Heath, 1977); and J. K. Friend, J. M. Power, and C. J. L. Yewlett, *Public Planning: The Inter-Corporate Dimension* (London: Tavistock Institute, 1974).

15. E. R. Alexander, "Policy Analysis," pp. 133-148 in Catanese and Snyder (eds.) op. cit.; A. Wildavsky, *Speaking Truth to Power: The Art and Craft of Policy Analysis* (Boston: Little-Brown, 1979); P. R. House, *The Art of Public Policy Analysis* (Beverly Hills, Calif.: Sage, 1982).

16. See, for example, G. E. Biles and S. R. Holmberg, *Strategic Human Resources Planning* (Glen Ridge, N.J.: Th. Horton & Daughters, 1980); A. Lauffer, *Social Planning at the Community Level* (Englewood Cliffs, N.J.: Prentice-Hall, 1978); and D. T. Shanahan and P. M. Wisenand, *The Dimensions of Criminal Justice Planning* (Boston: Allyn and Bacon, 1980).

17. Some of these, like the Model Cities Agencies of the late 1960s and early 1970s and LEAA of the mid and late 1970s, experienced an almost meteoric rise and fall, closely linked to federal funding. Others, like the Health Systems Agencies, seem to respond to an ongoing need, and have developed some stability and capacity for survival.

18. This question is discussed more extensively in A. Wildavsky, "If Planning is Everything, Maybe It's Nothing," *Policy Sciences* 4(2) (Summer 1973): 127-153; E. R. Alexander, "If Planning Isn't Everything, Maybe It's Something," *Town Planning Review* 52(2) (April 1981): 131-142; E. Reade, "Response," and E. R. Alexander, "Rejoinder," *Town Planning Review* 53(11) (January 1982): 65-78.

19. See J. Friedmann, "A Conceptual Model for the Analysis of Planning Behavior," *Administrative Science Quarterly* 12(3) (September 1967): 225-252; and G. Benveniste, *The Politics of Expertise* (Berkeley, Calif.: Glendessary Press, 1972), on which the following typology is based.

20. For examples, see A. Altschuler, *The City Planning Process: A Political Analysis* (Ithaca, N.Y.: Cornell University Press, 1965); A. J. Catanese, *Planners and Local Politics: Impossible Dreams* (Beverly Hills, Calif.: Sage, 1974). The tool of regulatory control is also an important aspect of comprehensive planning, which is discussed below.

21. National planning systems are described and evaluated in several studies; for a comparison of Great Britain and the U.S., see M. Clawson and P. Hall, *Planning and Urban Growth: An Anglo-American Comparison* (Baltimore: Johns Hopkins University Press, 1973); for Israel, see E. R. Alexander, R. Alterman, and H. Law-Yone, "Evaluating Plan Implementation: The Statutory Planning System in Israel," Vol. 20(2) of *Progress in Planning* (D. R. Diamond and J. B. McLoughlin, eds.) (Oxford: Pergamon, 1982); another comparative study is L. S. Bourne, *Urban Systems—Strategies for Regulation: A Comparison of Policies in Britain, Sweden, Australia, and Canada* (Oxford: Clarendon Press, 1975).

22. See, for example, J. Hayward and M. Watson (eds.), *Planning, Politics and Public Policy: The British, French and Italian Experience* (London: Cambridge University Press, 1975).

23. D. Listokin, *Fair Share Housing Allocation* (New Brunswick, N.J.: Center for Urban Policy Research-Rutgers University, 1976); D. Bryant, C. Chin, and W. C. Baer, *Fair Sharing: The State of the Art* (Springfield, Va.: NTIS, 1980).

24. For example, in A. Waterston, *Development Planning: Lessons of Experience*, (Baltimore: Johns Hopkins University Press, 1965); R. L. Meier, *Developmental Planning* (New York: McGraw-Hill, 1965).

25. See N. V. Giannis, *Economic Development: Thoughts and Problems* (N. Quincy, Mass.: Christopher Publishing, 1978), 84-110.

26. See, for example, D. A. Rondinelli (ed.), *Planning Development Projects* (Stroudsberg, Penn.: Dowden, Hutchinson & Ross, 1977).

27. D. N. Rothblatt, *Regional Planning: The Appalachian Experience* (Lexington, Mass.: D. C. Heath, 1971).

28. If *Le Plan* is credited with France's economic achievements, it also has to be blamed for failures; however, later assessments suggest that both were largely the result of broader, transnational, economic trends; see S. S. Cohen, *Modern Capitalist Planning: The French Model* (Berkeley, Calif.: California Press, 1977).

29. The best exposition of the comprehensive planning approach is found in M. C. Branch (ed.), *Urban Planning Theory* (Stroudsburg, Penn.: Dowden, Hutchinson & Ross, 1975).

30. For a more detailed comparison of comprehensive planning with other planning models, see S. S. Fainstein and N. I. Fainstein, "City Planning and Political Values," *Urban Affairs Quarterly*, 6 (March 1971): 341-362.

31. J. Friedmann, "The Future of Comprehensive Urban Planning: A Critique," *Public Administration Review* 31 (May-June 1971): 315-326; H. J. Gans, *People and Plans: Essays on Urban Problems in Solutions* (New York: Basic Books, 1968).

32. One exposition of social planning is that of A. J. Kahn, *Theory and Practice of Social Planning* (New York: Russell Sage, 1969).

33. J. W. Dyckman, "Social Planning, Social Planners, and Planned Societies," *Journal of the American Institute of Planners*, 26 (March 1960): 66-76.

34. P. Davidoff, "Advocacy and Pluralism in Planning," *Journal of the American Institute of Planners*, 31 (November 1965): 331-338.

35. Accounts of these efforts include: E. M. Blecher, *Advocacy Planning for Urban Development* (New York: Praeger, 1970); and M. Kaplan, "Advocacy and Urban Planning," *Social Welfare Forum* (New York: Columbia University Press, 1968), 58-77.

36. D. F. Maziotti, "The Underlying Assumptions of Advocacy Planning: Pluralism and Reform," *Journal of the American Institute of Planners*, 40 (January 1974): 38-48.

37. See, for example, F. F. Piven, et al., "Symposium: Whom Does the Advocacy Planner Serve?," *Social Policy* (May-June 1970): 32-37.

38. D. A. Barr, "The Professional Urban Planners," *Journal of the American Institute of Planners*, 38 (May 1972): 155-159.

39. J. K. Friend, and W. N. Jessop, *Local Government and Strategic Choice*, (London: Tavistock, 1969); S. S. Cohen, op. cit.

40. R. Goodman, *After the Planners* (New York: Simon & Schuster, 1971); R. Sennet, *The Uses of Disorder* (New York: Random House, 1970); S. Grabow and

A. Heskin, "Foundations for a Radical Concept of Planning," *Journal of the American Institute of Planners* 39 (March 1973): 106-114; J. Friedmann, *The Good Society: A Primer of Its Social Practice* (Los Angeles, Calif.: University of California School of Architecture and Urban Planning, 1976); P. M. Clavel, J. Forester, and W. J. Goldsmith (eds.), *Urban and Regional Planning in an Age of Austerity* (New York: Pergamon, 1980).

41. D. Braybrooke and C. E. Lindblom, *A Strategy of Decision: Policy Evaluation as a Social Process* (Glencoe, Ill.: Free Press, 1963).

42. B. H.Siegan, *Land Use Without Zoning* (Lexington, Mass.: D. C. Heath, 1973); R. Banham, et al., "Non-Plan: An Experiment in Freedom," *New Society*, 338 (March 1969).

43. See, for example, A. S. Travis, "Planning as Applied Ecology: The Management of Alternative Futures," *Town Planning Review* 48(1) (January 1977): 5-16; and R. L. Meier, "Preservation: Planning for the Survival of Things," *Futures* (April 1980): 128-141.

44. The technician-administrator role is compared to other, more political roles in different contexts in Altshuler, op. cit., and by F. F. Rabinowitz, *City Politics and Planning* (New York: Atherton, 1969); see also, J. L. Kaufman, "The Planner as Interventionist in Public Policy Issues," pp. 179-200 in Burchell and Sternlieb op. cit. for an exploration of planners' political roles and strategies.

45. See Alexander and Kaeser, op. cit.

46. M. L. Needleman and C. E. Needleman, *Guerillas in the Bureaucracy: The Community Planning Experiment in the U.S.* (New York: Wiley, 1974).

47. W. C. Baer, "Urban Planners: Doctors or Midwives," *Public Administration Review*, 37(6) (November-December 1977): 671-677.

48. M. F. Krieger, *Advice and Planning* (Philadelphia: Temple University Press, 1981), 191.

49. ibid., p. 192.

50. For example, A. Schutz, *The Phenomenology of the Social World* (G. Walsh and F. Lehner, eds.) (Evanston, Ill.: Northwestern University Press, 1967); L. Spurling, *Phenomenology and the Social World* (London: Routledge and Kegan-Paul, 1977).

51. R. Bernstein, *The Restructuring of Social and Political Theory* (Philadelphia: University of Pennsylvania Press, 1976); J. Habermas, *Knowledge and Human Interests* (Boston: Beacon Press, 1971); ibid., *Theory and Practice* (Boston: Beacon Press, 1973); P. Berger and T. Luckman, *The Social Construction of Reality* (New York: Anchor Press, 1966).

52. See J. Forrester, op. cit.; R. S. Bolan, "The Practitioner as Theorist: The Phenomenology of the Professional Episode," *Journal of the American Planning Association*, 46(3) (July 1980): 261-274.

53. Forrester, op. cit.; Bolan, op. cit., pp. 272-273; N. Patricios, "An Agentive Perspective of Urban Planning," *Town Planning Review*, 50(1) (January 1979): 36-54.

CHAPTER 5

Why Plan? — and Other Questions

In Chapter 2 we explored different views of planning, in search of a usable definition. Unavoidably, our search touched on the question of why planning is undertaken at all, but this was peripheral to our central concern. In concluding this review of current thinking about planning, we return to this question, and related ones: What is the rationale for planning? What can be the scope of planning, and what are its limits? What allows planners to plan and propose futures for others? The answers to these questions vary, according to whom you ask, but some of these answers come together to form an image of planners as they see themselves, on the one hand, or a view of planning, on the other hand, as seen by society.

The Rationale for Planning

"Why plan?" is a moot question in most of the conditions under which planning takes place. We have seen that planning can be viewed as a part of any activity that is more than an instinctive reflex. But more particularly, planning is an essential component of every social decision. Each societal unit, whether it is a family, group, organization, or government, is engaged in planning whenever it makes decisions or develops policies to change something on its own makeup or its environment. We seldom ask whether we should plan; planning takes place all the time.

Authority and Expertise

Naturally, not all planning is carried out by planners, nor should it be. However, when planning is undertaken by public planners rather than private individuals, what are the reasons for delegating this function to them as specialists? Legitimacy is a precursor of authority, authority for planners being that which enables them to evaluate and recommend choices between courses of action that will affect many others.

Planners have traditionally been accepted as design-oriented professionals. Their expertise has expanded to include the ability to aggregate diverse needs into a set of strategies to meet common objectives and goals. Planning, in this sense, is seen as the ability to apply the tools of rationality to the development of public policy.[1] Central to this process of aggregation is the concept of a definable public interest to which we will return.

Professional expertise is a widely recognized source of authority. Unfortunately, it is not always enough to win acceptance for planners' proposals in the political arena. The independence of the expert can be a forecaster of impotence, for the power to propose is rarely followed by the authority to implement.[2]

Another source of authority for the planner is bureaucratic position. In the bureaucratic role, planners get their authority from the elected officials of the government they serve. This legitimacy, however, is limited by several factors. Political officials may not be as broadly representative as they should be, so that they respond to the interest groups that elected them rather than to "the public interest." Furthermore, the theoretical distinction between the policymaking master and the administrative servant is blurred in practice, where many policy decisions are in fact made at the administrative level rather than by the legislative body.

A third base for planning authority is user preferences. In a kind of market model, the planner is seen as purveying planning services to diverse interests to meet different expressed needs. The social planning model demands that clients' needs be discovered scientifically, by surveys and other research or by user participation. The advocacy planning model holds that interests will be expressed through a political market. What these approaches have in common is basing planning legitimacy on participation in the decision-making process. Later, we shall discuss in more detail the relationship between planning and participation, and how it plays itself out in different contexts.

Lastly, planners' professional values can be a source of authority. In this view, planning is a value-laden profession, and the planner's internalization of values gives him or her the sanction to plan for others. The difficulty with this legitimation is that it holds good only as long as value consensus exists, or values are shared in a homogeneous community of planners and planned-for.

Reviewing this issue, Martin Rein suggests that:

> There are multiple sources of legitimacy, [which] cannot all be pursued under the auspices of one planning organization and hence choice is required...Each...has its characteristic weaknesses and strengths which present to the planner a set of intractable problems that are moral in character.[3]

When we explore planners' values and their self-image, we shall see how planners today, in fact, address these "intractable problems."

Planning and the Market

We view planning here as an integral part of any deliberate societal activity; therefore the rationale for planning is linked to social action. "Why plan?" is transformed into a question about the times and conditions when society should undertake deliberate action. Most social processes occur without such intervention. Family formation and population change, migration and resettlement, and industrialization and technological development have seldom been the result of any conscious decisions. These are powerful social movements, but they are in one sense simply the combination of an infinite number of decisions made by individuals and larger societal units.

The individual decisions and actions that constitute major social trends are of course planned. But they are planned and undertaken in the interests of the specific individual, household, or firm involved. Together they may be beneficent, as when millions of individual purchasing decisions are made with confidence that consumers will have more money to spend, and a market boom is generated. On the other hand, the aggregate self-interest can be unwittingly and systematically destructive.

Garret Hardin called this phenomenon "the tragedy of the commons." He drew an analogy with the destruction of common grazing enclosures in the medieval English village. Without regard for his neighbor's actions or the cumulative effect over time, each householder made the reasonable decision to graze as many cattle on the commons as possible, since the land cost him nothing. As a result, the commons were destroyed by overgrazing, and all the users were left poorer than before. A simple rationing

system might have preserved this public resource for the general benefit.[4]

The "tragedy of the commons" was brought about by the effect of
externalities, that is, by the external or spillover effects of one individual's
or unit's actions on others. A modern "tragedy of the commons" is central
city or neighborhood decline, evident in dilapidation and abandonment of
housing, widespread disinvestment, and eventual breakdown of social networks and norms. Again, the individual decisions of the family that de-
fers spending hard-earned cash on maintenance or repairs on which their
eventual return is uncertain, or of the landlord who abandons property
that yields less in rent than he owes in taxes, are rational. But the premises
on which these decisions were made—the low expected equity of the house
in the family's case, and the low rents in the landlord's—are themselves
the results of similar decisions made by their predecessors, decisions that
are part of a spiral of effects that often requires public intervention to
reverse.

Environmental pollution is another classic contemporary example of
external effects. The discharge from a brewery, which pollutes the down-
stream reaches of a river is not included in the cost of making the beer,
but it is a cost nevertheless, which is borne by the communities that have
to treat the river water to make it drinkable again. Similarly, the costs of
cleaning up a toxic waste site left by a chemical plant, or the effects on
surrounding neighborhoods of smoke emissions from a steel foundry, are
called "externalities." They are "externalities" because they have not been
included in the costs of production that are passed on to the direct consumer in competition with other producers. Unbridled competition provides an incentive for such externalities, so public intervention is required
to forestall such effects by regulation (as is done through zoning, and
through environmental controls, for example) or to internalize their costs
(as occurs when industrial polluters are charged for treatment or cleanup
costs).

The free market may founder on other obstacles. An example is the
emergence of monopolies. The local telephone company is a monopoly;
once one company has set up its network in a community, the cost of in-
stalling a parallel system prevents other firms from competing in the same
area. To prevent such monopolies from setting outrageously high prices in
the absence of competition, governments have regulated them as public
utilities. A different set of legal tools applies to oligopoly—the tendency
for a few large firms to dominate production and/or pricing of a class of
goods.

Some goods, however, are produced by governments and public organizations. They are distributed by means not recognized by the free market model. Public goods, such as defense or public safety, benefit everyone; like rain, they descend upon the just and the unjust alike. But they cannot be restricted to only those users who pay for them. If a few shopkeepers on a main street, for example, hired a private security force to patrol the street and ensure the safety of their stores and their clients, other firms in the area would also benefit, without sharing in the costs. This would put them at a competitive advantage, unless a governmental body intervened and used its legal authority to distribute the cost of these and similar services through taxation or assessments.

Merit goods, of which education is an example, confer a greater benefit on the individual than he or she may be willing or able to pay for. Because of the long-term benefit to society, a merit good may have to be provided below cost, with the deficit made up indirectly through taxes. This is why governments support symphony orchestras, for example, and provide subsidies for mass transit. A social consensus, as expressed in legislation, has recognized that the direct consumers of these services cannot pay their entire costs. Accordingly, if it were left to the free market, symphony orchestras would die out and mass transit would go bankrupt. But the social consensus has also recognized that there are indirect social benefits from these activities that transcend their direct value: The symphony orchestra contributes to the community's overall cultural heritage, while mass transit supports other social and economic activities by providing access to jobs for workers and access to retail and other services for potential users. In all of these situations social intervention may be justifiable to remedy the dysfunctions of the free market, and every social intervention of this kind involves planning.[5]

An alternative response to perceived failures in free market societies is to institute a planned economy. This is what socialism advocates, and it has been accomplished in Eastern Europe, China, and several countries of the Third World. Directed economies such as these could be seen as victories for planning were it not for their limitations, which include the sacrifice of some of the advantages of free markets.

The advantages and limitations of the free market and planned social intervention are summarized by Ralf Dahrendorff. Both market and plan, he agrees, are rational types of social organization. The market is efficient as a mechanism for transmitting individual wants and needs and is highly adaptable to conditions of uncertainty and change. But if society does not accept the existing distributions of power, resources, and participation, then the market must be supplemented by planned decisions that reflect societal values. These decisions are made through the political system.

Planned rationality is a mechanism for making deliberate social decisions, guided by purposeful social norms. Unlike the market, where individual, firm, and household decisions are created from the bottom up, the planned economy requires that planning proceed from the top down. Consequently, it depends heavily on predictions and projections and has to assume a large measure of certainty and stability. This makes centrally planned societies unstable and inefficient, as witnessed in Russia's agricultural production or China's "Great Leap Forward."[6]

Some claim, however, that planning is unnecessary even for those decisions that are beyond the scope of the open—economic—market, and that have to be taken by the political system. Charles Lindblom has long held that the interplay of individual and organizational decisions in the political arena, just as in the economic one, will produce outcomes which are superior, for society at large, than any that can be devised by deliberate planned intervention. For this type of decision making, he coined the term "disjointed incrementalism" (which we have referred to before), while he called this type of interaction, or self-coordination, between organizations "partisan mutual adjustment."[7] However, "disjointed incrementalism" has some serious defects as a mode of social decision making: It has a conservative bias that tends to perpetuate the status quo, it is incapable of generating solutions, and, therefore, it cannot be used in unstable or rapidly changing situations or in response to any novel problem or crisis.[8] As a result, while it is widely conceded that "disjointed incrementalism" is a realistic description of how decision making occurs in many situations,[9] serious questions remain about whether it really is a "good" way to go about making decisions.

Another way of describing the tension between planning and decision making in the political marketplace is Wildavsky's contrast between "pure planning"—or "analysis as an intellectual construct," which he calls "intellectual cogitation"—and "analysis as social interaction" or "pure politics." Wildavsky concedes the need for both: "if analysis were purely intellectual, analysts would be everything, or if analysis were purely interactive, analysts would be nothing." But he dismisses planning by equating it to the "ideal type" of pure rationality, a type impossible to realize, of course, in the flesh-and-blood world of conflicting interests, political decisions, and concrete action.[10]

Planning today, however, is a far cry from the "straw-man" of pure rational analysis described by Wildavsky. The planning model and roles presented above reflect the disintegration of the "scientific-rational" comprehensive planning approach of the 1950s and early 1960s. They suggest a concern with the realities of political interactions, an appreciation of human and organizational relationships, and a consciousness of the need to link plans with implementation and action, which was absent before. Planning today, as it is conceived of by many of those thinking about it, and as it is carried out by its best practitioners, is becoming just a hybrid between intellectual cogitation—rational analysis—and social interaction—recognizing and interacting with the planner's political context—that Wildavsky suggests is needed for effective input into the policymaking process.

Planning: Its Scope and Limits

In presenting the rationale for planning, we have also said something about its scope. In the private arena, planning is invoked whenever foresight is necessary to reduce uncertainty, and when anticipation is required to cope with the complexity of final action. In the public arena, planning provides the basis for rational collective action. Planned public intervention is required, at a minimum, in connection with the basic functions of government: preserving public security, reducing external friction, maintaining general prosperity, and reducing internal frictions between the different groups and interests that make up a country's society.[11]

The preceding discussion has also displayed some of the arguments against planning, suggesting, if just by inference, that planning can only occur within strict limits. If we have explored the scope of planning we should also investigate its limits in more detail for a sensible balance between aspirations and reality. Two types of limits can be identified. The first can be called intrinsic limits: constraints imposed by the nature of the planning process itself, and are universal wherever planning is attempted. The second are contextual limits: situational factors that may make planning difficult or impossible.

Intrinsic Limits

Just as planning is an organizational and social response to uncertainty, so uncertainty itself sets intrinsic limits to planning. Three types of such limits correspond to three kinds of uncertainty in the planning process.[12] The first is limited knowledge, empirical or theoretical, linking causes and effects. The engineer has no difficulty constructing a machine to convert fuel energy into movement, for example, because of our extensive knowledge of physics, combined with mechanics, metallurgy, and so on. Social engineering, however, is more problematic. Some planning interventions seemed simple, such as the construction of freeways to provide accessibility and address subsequent traffic congestion, until unintended consequences revealed the narrow scope of our essentially technical knowledge.

Seemingly technical issues are sometimes ambiguous from the start, due to conflicting interpretations of empirical evidence. Examples of this kind of uncertainty are the controversies over the SST and over nuclear power production. Finally, there are many areas of social intervention where theory, information, and experience are still very hazy about what causes which effects. Economists are still locked in dispute, for example, on the causes of inflation, recession, and unemployment, as are social scientists on the reasons for poverty, crime, and discrimination. Any program or project premised on a particular set of assumptions linking causes and effects in these areas is just as likely to fail as it is to succeed.[13]

The second is uncertainty about institutional frameworks and the organizational environment, and its responses to the planning process and its outcomes. Here we are not talking about how changing, uncertain, and turbulent the actual organizational environment may be—that will come later; reference is to planners' lack of knowledge about their own and other relevant organizations, and their inability to predict accurately how they will interact. In its simplest form, this is the uncertainty whether a zoning appeals committee will adopt or reject the planning staff's recommendations. In more complex forms, this uncertainty leads to unplanned outcomes such as the dilution of the Model Cities Program in the United States.[14] In response to our ignorance in this area, a whole new field of study is emerging, which is looking at how policies and programs are implemented by complex networks involving many different organizations. We have come to realize that most bureaucracies are, in fact, such networks, and that most planned undertakings need some kind of coordination to be successful.[15]

The third area of uncertainty is the difficulty of predicting future values, goals, and objectives in light of accelerating social change. On the one hand, some stability in goals and values—certainly enough to make planning possible—is an essential prerequisite for the existence and integrity of social institutions and organizations, and for any kind of deliberate collective action.[16] A city cannot designate a right-of-way for a highway, and plan and design the arterial, if it has little confidence that people will want or need automobile transportation after the four or five years it takes to implement such a proposal, and over the decade or two during which its construction must be amortized. The state will have difficulty deciding on a site for a power plant, if its planners do not know whether people will, in fact, be using electricity twenty years into the future, or whether, instead, we will have all retired to Amish-style preindustrial communes by then or, alternatively, have emigrated to solar-powered satellite communities.

However, within the extremes of these far-fetched alternatives, a wide range of uncertainty still prevails. The stub ends of discontinued freeways are evidence of a profound change in values that few anticipated, as is the return to central cities, which is already creating problems of "gentrification" in areas that were written off during the heyday of suburban development. These uncertainties, endemic to decision making in general, affect planning in particular because of its future orientation. Given their scale and complexity, the lead times of more and more undertakings, which may exceed twenty years in cases such as nuclear power plants or statewide infrastructure networks like the California Water Plan, make this problem critical.

Planning, then, is intrinsically limited in its potential to address organizational and social problems. These limits are set by uncertainty about the relations between cause and effect in our environment, ignorance of possible organizational and institutional behavior and interactions, and the instability of the values, goals, and objectives of the people we are planning for. Especially the last, increasingly critical in a changing and complex society, raises the specter of unanticipated outcomes to well-meant interventions.[17] Unfortunately, there is no way in which this constraint can be overcome, because

> Ideas and values are significant areas of indeterminancy, and the same goes for meanings. These are only generated in confrontation with reality, and therefore they cannot be predicted.[18]

Contextual Limits

Besides the intrinsic limits described above, various contexts may s additional constraints on planned collective action. Basically, these c textual constraints are the results of the characteristics of political tems. Consequently, there may be differences in how effectively pl can perform between one context and another, which is related to

ferences between their respective systems of government, political, social, and economic values, and systems of institutionalization.

Sir Geoffrey Vickers has suggested that a political system is "constituted by those relations which a society seeks to regulate by the exercise of public power."[19] The degree to which societies deploy public power to regulate relations, then, is one difference in their political contexts which may be very relevant to the utilization and effectiveness of planning. Even a superficial comparison between the United States, for example, on the one hand, the "welfare states" or social democracies of Western Europe (such as Britain, France, the Netherlands, the Scandinavian nations, and West Germany) on the other, will suggest that in the former planning will encounter greater obstacles than in the latter. This is confirmed, for example, if we examine, in retrospect, the "Great Society" programs. America's last great experiment with social legislation and public intervention.[20]

The stability or instability of social and political systems, too, may set contextual limits on planning. The uncertain environments of many Third World countries, for example—both internally and externally—often make systematic long-range planning difficult if not impossible. Under these conditions, many "plans" that are produced are quite irrelevant to real-life circumstances, and the rational planning process becomes an exercise in futility.[21]

Developed countries, too, may not be immune from instabilities, turbulence, and change that threaten effective planning. Different nations are affected in different ways at different times, but a trend was predicted for Western societies over a decade ago, which appears no less relevant today. This is the tendency for destabilizing changes to be initiated by the economic market and technological innovations, which, though accepted as unavoidable, create the need for more regulation and intervention. Environmental pollution or protection, energy consumption or conservation, and population policy, are just three areas in which this phenomenon is ~arent. But a society's capacity to regulate itself is limited, and shrinks ⸱he traditional authority of government is challenged, and when con- ⸱een various interests is eroded by open conflict.[22] The chal- ⸱ning modes of planning that can cope with conditions of and change has stimulated some thinkers,[23] but it is ⸱ practice has yet to meet.

ᴠhy plan?," we could not help touching the

related issue of why planners should plan. What entitles planners to plan for others? What are the sources of their legitimacy? When discussing planners authority as professional experts in aggregating collective decisions we used the term the common public interest. This concept has long been considered one source of planning legitimacy. On the other hand, if the public interest, as manifested in a rational planning process, presents problems, another source of legitimacy is available: participation. Participation in the planning process of those who are to be its beneficiaries, can provide a constituency for planning and legitimize the proposals of the plan. Finally, the goals and values of the planners themselves could justify their special role in the planning process.

The Public Interest

The rational planning approach and the traditional model of comprehensive planning are both premised on the idea that there is a collective "public interest" that can be identified through the planning process, and becomes the criterion for evaluating alternative planning proposals. This "public interest" represents the aggregation of all the values of the community, or the agreed-upon set of goals and objectives toward which the rational planning process is expected to work. The existence of such a public interest was taken for granted during the heyday of comprehensive planning, "rational" administration and "good" government through the 1930s to the 1950s, and the ability of planners and administrators, working with elected officials, to identify this public interest and justify their proposals in its name, was rarely questioned.

However, as problems grew more complex and different groups became more explicit in their demands, the approach of addressing urban problems piecemeal on the basis of such an assumed consensus seemed less and less satisfactory.[24] In theory, too, the concept of "the public interest" came under attack by the "pluralist" school of thought, so-named because of their idea that political decisions are the result of an interplay of different, or plural, interests. They came to the conclusion that:

> there is no public interest theory worthy of the name and that the concept itself is significant primarily as a datum of politics. . .it may. . .be nothing more than a label attached indiscriminately to a miscellany of particular compromises of the moment.[25]

This conclusion became accepted wisdom during the 1960s and 1970s among theorists and practitioners of social planning and advocacy planing, and among proponents of more radical planning approaches. However, at the same time comprehensive planning, as institutionalized in local, regional, and state government and planning agencies, and sectoral planning, as prescribed by a host of federal programs, continued to be practiced as if a public interest did exist. Both in the federal-state-local intergovernmental "marble cake" of the United States and similar federated countries, and in the more hierarchical systems of other, more centralized, polities such as Great Britain, the Netherlands, and Sweden, planning continues to be practiced in a broad range of areas—from air quality to zoning—on the assumption, sometimes borne out in fact, that planning analysis and rational interaction with officials and elected representatives can identify a public interest and work toward its realization.

In spite of its demolition by the pluralists, the public interest in planning practice is alive and well. In theory, too, the case has been made that the public interest can still be a valid legitimizer of planned action, and a useful criterion for planning proposals, even when we recognize the politcal nature of planning and public decisions. This view joins the pluralists in discarding the "old" public interest, which is based on an image of planning as objective, scientific, and value-free. It acknowledges—indeed welcomes—the normative nature of planning; that is, planning as a process of deciding what will be, in the light of preferences and values. In this sense, a public interest can be ascertained. This can be done through a rational analysis of values, even if they are of conflicting groups and interests, by adopting an explicit value criterion, such as: "give everyone the greatest liberty possible," or, "first improve the lot of those who are worst off."[26]

In another perspective, still relating to planning as a normative activity, the public interest could be identified as the interests of relevant individuals and groups in the collectivity. Naturally, this begs the question of who is relevant and who is not, but even if this is decided in a political arena, the concept can serve in the planning process as a framework for collecting and presenting data on the impacts of alternative proposals on various affected parties.[27] In fact, some of the evaluative methods referred to above, such as environmental impact statements, the planning balance sheet, and the goals-achievement matrix, implicitly adopt this public interest criterion.

Finally, we could adopt a procedural perspective to identify a public interest. In this view, one could say that a planning process and its outcomes are in the public interest if all the affected groups have had access to the planning process and have been involved in making the relevant decisions.[28] This view of the public interest, of course, leads directly to another legitimator of planning: public participation.)

Public Participation

Ever since local planning became institutionalized, public participation has been invoked to give planning the quality of "due process" demanded of rational administrative and political decision making. Public participation means the involvement in the planning process of all the individuals, groups, interests, organizations, and communities who might be affected by its outcomes. This is more than indirect participation through representative elected officials, or appointed administrators who are assigned to a liaison role to find out and communicate the relevant parties' needs and goals. It means direct interaction, in the context of developing, reviewing, and adopting plans and proposals, between the planners and responsible officials, and the affected parties themselves.

In planning, public participation has traditionally taken the form of open hearings on planning proposals and the consideration of any objections received after due notice of proposals has been given to the public. While participation requirements in U.S. federally funded programs were already mandated by the Housing Act of 1954,[29] it was the 1960s that became "the decade of participation" with inclusion of the "maximum feasible participation" requirement in the Community Action and the Model Cities programs.[30]

(Public participation—also referred to as community participation or citizen participation, depending on one's ideological orientation—can serve a variety of purposes. These may be different from differing points of view. (From the planner's, administrator's, or official's perspective, citizen participation may be designed to involve the public at large in the planning process and thus increase their trust in government and their identification with the resulting decisions. People with an opposing point of view would label this "tokenism" and suggest, instead, that communities are demanding a real voice in planning, and want better plans, decisions, and public services.[31] As the perspectives on public participation vary, its objectives vary too, and may range from redistributing power, through reducing peoples' alienation from the political system, to educating citizens and providing them with information.) A wide array of techniques has been deployed to realize these objectives: it includes meetings, hearings, citizen boards, advisory councils or task forces, citizen surveys, charettes, games and simulations, and employing citizens or neighborhood residents in intermediary or paraprofessional capacities.[32]

Many of the aspirations of public participation are unexceptionable: who could disagree with the goals of improving the quality of decision making, for example, or of offering the individual citizen an opportunity for self-fulfillment in the context of the political system? But there are also problems. The participation mechanisms employed may fit one set of goals, the administration's, say, but not the other, the community's (or vice versa), and many of the objectives are mutually incompatible. For example, hearings may be highly suitable for providing citizens with information, but they are hardly likely to contribute to their sense of power or involvement in the decision-making process. On the other hand, an elected citizen task force with authority to review and affect planning decisions may give a community a sense of power, but it is uncertain whether it will, in fact, improve the quality of decisions or enhance public services. In short, process-related and task-related objectives may well conflict.[33]

Over the years, a substantial body of experience in public participation, which has been the subject of some study and evaluation, has accumulated. What have been the impacts of participation, and what factors have contributed to its success or failure? Some studies suggest that participation can have a positive impact on the quality of public services delivery, but that it may be limited or only over the short-term. On real power redistribution between citizens and the political, bureaucratic, planning, and administrative "establishment" the findings are mixed, but there is a good deal of agreement that gaining access to the decision-making apparatus is not easy. While citizen participation has sometimes succeeded in mobilizing previously unheard interests, these may be of all persuasions, from "rednecks" to "radicals." The impacts of participation on citizen attitudes have been slight, on the whole, while its costs have sometimes been felt in the form of less efficient policymaking and increased conflict.[34] In fact, there is still little evidence that the mass of the public at large really wants to participate enough to surmount the considerable obstacles in its way.[35] After all, most people, and especially working men and women, have other things on their minds, and more important claims on their time, than participating in a meeting called to review the quality of city services in their neighborhood, or to affect the county's decision on where to locate a new hospital. It usually takes the perception of a crisis directly affecting their daily lives, such as the prospect of a tavern moving

in next door in a quiet residential area, or the threat of closing the neighborhood school, or a fatality on an accident-prone street intersection in a
central-city community, to mobilize people to invest the time, effort, and
organization that will enable them to affect and change public decisions.

None of the experience has suggested any sure-fire formula for success,
but a central factor in cases where citizens gained any effective input into
decision making has been organization. The format that has seemed most
successful has been the formalization of citizen involvement in decisions
affecting their neighborhood or community through an elected board with
formal authority.[36] However, this conclusion must be qualified: successful
for whom, and in achieving which of participation's many possible objectives?

This remains the dilemma, too, of planners invoking citizen participation to legitimize the planning process. In mobilizing a constituency is
the planner an advocate or a manipulator—a "servant of the people" or
someone coopting others to implement his own values, carry out a government's plan, or defuse conflict to maintain the status quo?[37] This question, ultimately, can only be answered subjectively, by the person involved in each particular case. It is important for the planner to ask the
question, however, and to have a critical consciousness of the meaning
of her involvement. The answer, of course, subjective as it must be, will
depend on the final legitimizer of planning: the planner's own values and
what he views as the goals of planning.

Goals and Values

One response to the question, "What is planning for?," holds that planning must be undertaken in situations where the forces of supply and
demand, as expressed through the market, fail to meet social needs. These
needs will be different, of course, in every case. However, is there a common goal or set of human needs at a higher level of abstraction that should
be the objective of any planning efforts?

Discussion of the goals and values implicit in planning has been surprisingly limited, in spite of their special relevance to planners. One might
assume that the most concrete articulation of goals would be the professional planners' code of ethics, but it is quite vague:

> A planner primarily serves the public interest and shall accept or
> continue employment only when the planner can insure accom-
> modation of the client's or employer's interest with the public
> interest.[38]

The public interest, of course, has been discussed above, and we have learned what a nebulous concept that can be. A suggestion of the values that constitute this public interest was offered by a group called Concerned Architects and Planners:

> The proper role of professional planners on issues of public policy does, we believe, require a commitment to certain basic common values, and we would hope that our profession would be united in its commitment to those values: humaneness, democracy, rationality.[39]

Professional ethics in planning, then, as in other professions, offer relatively little help in articulating the profession's values. Even when those values are humaneness, democracy, and rationality, the planning code of ethics is too oriented toward the "client-serving, guild-related roles of planners to examine their real effect on the social, economic, and political system in which the planners' activities take place."[40]

The term public interest is too vague, and humaneness, democracy, rationality, perhaps too culture-specific, to serve as planning's ultimate goal. Striving to synthesize a range of planning objectives, Faludi proposed that the goal of planning is the encouragement of human growth.[41] This is based on the idea, presented by the psychologist-philosopher Abraham Maslow, that human needs exist in a hierarchy that ranges from the basic material needs of food and shelter, through psychological needs such as love and security, to the highest need of each individual for personal fulfillment. Promoting human growth, then, ensures that needs will be met at each level of this hierarchy.

As an end for planning, the enhancement of human growth is laudable; it subsumes all other objectives. Human growth should be the ultimate goal not only of planning but of all social activity. On the other hand, this vastness of purpose makes this end less than satisfactory as a practical goal for a profession. No distinction is possible between planning and any other type of thought or action. There is no yardstick by which to evaluate planners' professional contributions and behavior. Human growth is too abstract, and, in concrete terms and contexts, one person's growth may be another's destruction.

An instructive approach to qualifying these broad definitions of planning goals is in another section of the professional Code of Ethics, which states:

> A planner shall seek to expand choice and opportunity for all per-

sons, recognizing a special responsibility to plan for the needs of disadvantaged groups and persons, and shall urge the alteration of policies, institutions, and decisions which militate against such objectives.

This approach has in fact served as a practical guideline for the planners who developed a policy plan for Cleveland, which concluded that:

Equity requires that government institutions give priority attention to the goal of promoting a wider range of choices for those Cleveland residents who have few, if any, choices.[42]

Maximizing choices for all and focusing on those whose choices are most limited may be as near to an operational objective for planning as is possible. The requirements for equity are tangible enough to serve as a yardstick for the evaluation of planning efforts and as a guide for identifying the public interest in comparing the impacts of policy options.[43]

John Friedmann has identified a set of planning goals appropriate to the changing postindustrial society of the United States and the developed West. In this context, says Friedmann, the emerging style of planning will have

To regard the future as open to choice and experimental action

To place the person as a source of moral values in the center of any action

To search for participant forms of social organization

To enlarge the scope for autonomous group action by. . .linking the new communitarian forms of social relations into larger participatory structures capable of sharing effectively in the processes of societal guidance.[44]

These goals can be viewed as complementary to those of the Cleveland group. Those would optimize society as it is, while Friedmann's goals are based on a changed society, or aim to change the present one. In Cleveland, a planning process is taken as given, and a criterion is developed for use in that context. Friedmann suggests that planning ought to aim at changing the planning process itself, and he proposes some objectives for a kind of planning that has yet to exist.

It is not surprising that there is no consensus yet on planning's values and goals; after all, no consensus exists on what planning is. As we begin to detect a convergence among definitions of planning, however, there is a chance for a synthesis of different goals. We agree that planning is a force

Planning in Change
Source: Hedman, *op. cit.*, pp. 4–5; copyright: permission (and plates) from Richard Hedman, San Francisco CA.

for change. Whether planners accomplish a change in society by maximizing choice, or whether a change of society forces them to consider Friedmann's proposed planning process, may in the end be a matter of circumstances rather than debate.

Problems and Prospects

This review will close with a look at some problems that planners are facing at present, and some of the prospects for planning in the future. To anyone reading this far, many problems are already apparent. The "classic" model of rationality, which has been the basic structure for planning and other management, administrative, and decision sciences, has been undermined for so long that it is crumbling, and only a scattering of puny "lean-to's" are rising to take its place. The planning mode which evolved through the first half of this century—"comprehensive planning"—is no longer the universal standard of practice. Though still widely applied in many planning agencies, it has been supplanted since the mid-1960s by rival models that today prevail in uneasy coexistence. Professional expertise, based on technical knowledge, is widely distrusted,[45] and the limits

of the role of technical expert or advisor are being recognized, even by planning practitioners themselves.[46] Today there is no single prescribed role for the planning professional, and planners must learn to live with ambiguity, uncertainty, and change. How have these problems affected planners? What is the planner's self-image, and what are the values which guide planning practitioners in their day-to-day decisions? Finally, what, in fact, is the role of planning in society today, and what are its prospects in the emerging society of tomorrow?

Planners: Their Practice, Self-Image, and Values

Through the 1950s and into the 1970s, the planning profession mushroomed, and by the mid-1970s "planning appears to have burst all over the map." Even the more "traditional" practitioners of planning, organized in the American Institute of Planners and the American Society of Planning Officials, grew from about 2,700 to some 22,000. However, by the early 1970s, the roles and approaches in practice of these planners had changed less than might have been expected, considering the radical changes that had taken place in planning theory and education. Planning agencies were still primarily oriented toward rational comprehensive planning, and their professional staff still saw themselves in technical advisory roles.[47]

By the end of the 1970s much of this had changed. Planners today are caught between incompatible models of planning and conflicting roles. On the one hand, they still feel a strong commitment to the ideals of rationality and comprehensiveness; on the other hand, they recognize the value-laden nature of planning and reject the pretensions of political neutrality implicit in the traditional "master plan." Nevertheless, many planners still see their roles as staff and technical advisors to elected executives, rather than as advocates for a given policy, and believe that rational comprehensive planning is compatible with a pluralistic society. This ambiguity of planning models and roles is accompanied by relative dislocation between basic personal value factors (such as utopianism or self-respect), professional value factors (such as effectiveness or comprehensiveness), and the decision strategies planners adopt in practice, which may range from rational to incremental.[48]

One way in which practicing planners today have adapted to this bind in which they find themselves is either to specialize in a particular role—the "technician" or the "politician"—or to become a "hybrid" and adopt either role as circumstances demand. The "hybrid" role, in fact, seems to be dominating planning practice. It is not too clear what the factors are that make a planner choose to become a "technician," "politician," or "hybrid." Personal variables, such as planners' ages or the kind of education they received, were thought to be important, but turned out to be insignificant. Instead, the planner's job setting seems to make the most difference. In large agencies, there is more room for specialization, and planning staff can select themselves into roles for which they feel most suitable. Consequently, these contexts reveal more "politicians" and "technicians," with many of the former in the larger cities. In smaller agencies, on the other hand, staff have to adapt to meet the varying demands of the job, so county and smaller local agencies contain more "hybrids."[49]

The ambiguity of planners' roles today also affects their personal and professional values and the way these are transformed into behavior in practice. The ethical values of planners have become relative rather than absolute, and the tactics, roles, and political orientations that the planner adopts relative to a particular issue in a given circumstances affect the degree to which she carries particular ethical norms (such as: do not divulge "inside" information) into practice. Though as a group they still have identifiable stands on particular questions—for example, they are more pro-environmental protection and pro-mass transit than the public at large—it is questionable how applicable the rigid ethics and value premises of the traditional planning profession are to planners' behavior in actual issues today.[50]

But perhaps this ambiguity is not all bad. We have experienced some of the defects of the traditional professional model, and some of the negative consequences—unanticipated, of course—of well-intentioned but overconfident professional intervention. Alternatively, the rigorous scientific expert or pure professional advisor could find himself doomed to impotence in a milieu of pragmatic political decisions. With all its ambiguities, today's planner's appraisal of her role is probably at once more responsible, and more realistic, than the more simplistic stereotypes of the past.

Planning in Society: The Present and the Future

Planning has come a long way since the hopes and expectations of its heyday just before and after World War II. Today it is unthinkable for someone to propose (and in the United States, at that!) that planning could become a "fourth branch of government."[51] Indeed, the wheel seems to have come full circle. In the political philosophy that has become increasingly prominent since the mid 1970s, and which dominates the current American administration, planning is almost a dirty word. In part, this reflects an even more widely held perception of impotence:

> Certainly, nothing proceeded according to desire. In the long run, failure was the only thing that worked predictably. All else was accidental. . .Solutions did not appear as readily as before, and things were not so clear as they once seemed. Things were just not working out as planned. Nothing ran smoothly. Nothing was succeeding as planned.
>
> "Nothing Succeeds as Planned" was the title of Gold's article. . . . Ralph called him at home the day after Gold mailed him four copies. . ."He was calling from the White House, " Dina said. . . "God, Bruce," Ralph began, "I can't tell you how you're boggling our minds. If nothing succeeds as planned—and you really present such a strong argument—then the President has just the excuse he needs for not doing anything."[52]

As we can see, the societal response to this sense of impotence may be inaction. In fact, history often shows a sequence of cycles—dynamic activism alternating with a more passive withdrawal into simpler and more limited loyalties. If we are in such a phase now, it is more than likely that a new cycle of dynamic intervention provoked by a prevading sense of crises that must be addressed, may be in the offing. In any case, impotence cannot lead to inaction: life must go on:

> Action is greater than inaction: perform therefore thy task in life. Even the life of the body could not be if there were not action.[53]

In the societal body, action is linked to collective decision, and decision demands planning.

Today, in ways that were undreamed of fifty years ago, planning has become imbedded in society. Many aspects of planning are so integrated in public decision making that they are now taken for granted. This is true for the physical form of local communities, where land-use planning and regulation is a fact of life recognized equally by residents, property owners, politicians, and developers. It is true for national programs, where analyses by agencies such as the Bureau of the Budget or the General Accounting Office, by independent "think tanks" like the Brookings Institute or the Rand Corporation, by private lobbies such as the Petroleum Institute or the Wilderness Society, or by consultants enlisted by public agencies and private interests alike accompany policy from its inception to its termination. In areas ranging from air pollution control to zero-lot-line zoning, and at all levels of government, planning has to provide the forward-looking basis of analysis, projection, and evaluation that becomes the underpinning for decision and action. In the private sector, too, long-run strategic planning is becoming increasingly important.[54]

It is clear, then, that the function of planning and planners' roles today are assured, even though there is disenchantment with what planning has accomplished, and a healthy skepticism about its potential. Not all job descriptions for planning or planning-related positions reflect their real content. Some may, indeed, have planning in their names; others may be called "fiscal analyst," "program evaluation," or by even less revealing names. But what they have in common is their involvement in the planning process (as described above) or in one or more of its stages, and the deployment of analysis, interaction, or a combination of both, to bring knowledge to bear on decision and action.

If there is disenchantment with what planning has achieved, it is in large measure justified. Planning was presented as capable of recasting society in a better mold, and it has not come close to accomplishing that. If there is cynicism about planning's potential for social change, it is warranted in the light of experience. Planning is an instrument serving the society that uses it, and, like any tool, it cannot perform more than the hand that wields it or the mind that controls it. It is a tool, however, that has come to serve society in small ways and great ones, and that is indispensible for organized life as we know it today.

In the future, the need for planning is going to be greater. Society shows no signs of becoming simpler or less complex; on the contrary. It is doubtful whether the limits of planning–the intrinsic ones of uncertainty, ignorance, and constraints on our capacity to handle even the information we have, and the contextual ones of organizational interactions, political systems, and social values–can stretch to meet these needs. Indeed, these may be the very brakes which slow down the spiral of change in technology, social organization, and human values that we have almost come to accept as a fact of life. But "small is beautiful" and "soft technology," though they may come to prevail in important spheres of life, will not eliminate the need for planning. Rather, the enhanced consciousness of many kinds of trade-off (such as between environmental and development values) that people were unaware of only a few decades ago, will only multiply the arenas where planning has to be undertaken before decisions can be made. Planners in the future will be found in virtually every niche of organized life and society. With a heightened sense of their responsibility, and with the consciousness of their frailty born of decades of planning experience, they are bound to be more effective than their counterparts today.

Discussion Questions and Exercises

1. Which of the following factors will require the intervention of planning and political decisions to adjust the "free" working of the market? Which of them may require such intervention (depending on your political-economic philosophy); which of them does not require any intervention?

   (a) Monopolies or oligopolies as a result of economies ~~~~~
   (b) "Natural" or locational monopolies;
   (c) Business failures during recessions or dep
   (d) The sequence of "boom" and "bust"
        business cycle;
   (e) Business failures as a result of entreprene

(f) Poverty as a result of unequal distribution of wealth/income;
(g) Assuring the supply of "public" and/or "merit" goods;
(h) Regulating and/or "internalizing" the effects of externalities.

2. Give an example from your reading and/or experience of each of the factors that you have identified as demanding or possibly needing planning intervention. Describe what form the planning intervention (if there has been any) has taken in each case.

3. If planning does not only mean public intervention, identify from your knowledge or experience other forms and arenas of planning. Why was planning needed in each of the cases you describe?

4. Which of the following has/have been invoked as sources for planners' authority to plan for others?

(a) Professional expertise and scientific analysis;
(b) Ability to identify and respond to needs and problems of client groups;
(c) Professional ethics and values;
(d) Working with communities in a joint participatory planning process;
(e) Filling a bureaucratic-administrative role;
(f) Advising government-elected representative officials;
(g) Appropriate political ideology;
(h) Empathy with groups being planned with/for.

5. With which of the arguments for planners' authority that you have identified under question 4 above do you agree, and which do you reject? Give the reasons for your conclusions;

6. Define the "public interest." Do you agree that such a concept exists? If it does, how can it be identified and used in planning? If it does not, what would you substitute as a rationale for comprehensive planning?

7. Do professional planners have a set of professional ethics—rules to which they are expected to conform? If so, where can they be found? If not, what does that imply for the claims of planning to be a pro-sion?

8. What is the role of "the public interest" in the professional ethics of planning (if any, and if there are such ethics)? If the "public interest" is included among planners' values, how has this value been operationalized? Describe an example and its impacts, if any.

9. What are some of the roles that professional planners have adopted, according to recent research? Which of the following factors affect the role choices of planners:

   (a) Age;
   (b) Sex;
   (c) Political ideology in general;
   (d) The specific issue involved + political orientation;
   (e) Job context—agency size;
   (f) Job context—geographic location of state;
   (g) Job context—large or small city.

10. What do you see as the future of planning? Describe the functions that planning might perform in the society of the future, and identify some emerging sectors that will call for planning and planners' skills. In which other sectors may planning become routinized and transformed into bureaucratic-administrative activities? Do you see yourself being involved in any of the planning-related roles you have described? If you do, give some of your reasons, and tell us how you would see yourself carrying out your planning activities.

Notes

1. John W. Dyckman, "The Practical Uses of Planning Theory," *Journal of the American Institute of Planners,* (September 1969): 299.
2. See, for example, A. Altshuler, op. cit., A. J. Catanese, op cit., and R. S. Bolan and R. L. Nuttall, *Urban Planning and Politics* (Lexington, Mass.: D. C. Heath, 1975); an insightful discussion of the role of planning expertise is G. Benevesite, op. cit.; see especially D. Eversley, *The Planner in Society: The Changing Role of a Profession* (Faber and Faber, 1973).
3. Martin Rein, "Social Planning: The Search for Legitimacy," *Journal of the American Institute of Planners* 35 (July 1969): 243.
4. Garrett Hardin, " The Tragedy of the Commons," *Science*, 162 (December 1968): 1243-1248.
5. An extensive body of literature in welfare economics deals with these issues. For a valuable concise rationale for planning based on these considerations, see T. Moore, op. cit.

6. Ralf Dahrendorff, "Market and Plan: Two Types of Rationality," in his *Essays in the Theory of Society* (Stanford, Calif.: Stanford University Press, 1968), 217-227.

7. Lindblom's work in this area spans nearly three decades, from "muddling through" in C. E. Lindblom, op. cit., to C. E. Lindblom, *Politics and Markets*, C. E. Lindblom, *The Intelligence of Democracy* (New York: Free Press, 1965).

8. Y. Dror, "Muddling Through: Science or Inertia," *Public Administration Review*, 24 (1964); A. Etzioni, "Mixed Scanning: A 'Third' Approach to Decision Making," *Public Administration Review*, 27 (1967): 387-391; E. R. Alexander, "Choice in a Changing World," *Policy Sciences*, 3(3) (September 1972): 325-337.

9. This has been well demonstrated especially in the context of budgeting decisions; see, for example, A. Wildavsky, *Budgeting: A Comparative Theory of Budgetary Processes* (Boston, Mass.: Little-Brown, 1975); for a broader review of incrementalism in the political arena, see G. C. Edwards, III and I. Sharkansky, *The Policy Predicament: Making and Implementing Public Policy* (San Francisco, Calif.: Freeman, 1978), 233-291. However, even as a description of the budgeting process, there are some doubts as to the universality of "incrementalism": See pp. 22,36 above.

10. A. Wildavsky (1979), op. cit., pp. 120-131.

11. C. K. Friedrich, "Political Development and the Objectives of Modern Government," in *Political and Administrative Development* (R. Braibanti, ed.) (Durham, N.C.: Duke University Press, 1969), 115-116.

12. Friend and Jessop, op. cit.; I. Masser, "The Limits of Planning," *Town Planning Review*, 51(1) (January 1980): 39-49.

13. For a stimulating description and illustrations of this and the other limits, see P. Hall, *Great Planning Disasters* (London: Wiedenfeld and Nicholson, 1980).

14. C. M. Haar, *Between the Idea and the Reality: A Study in the Origin, Fate and Legacy of the Model Cities Program* (Boston, Mass.: Little-Brown, 1975); B. J. Frieden and M. Kaplan, *The Politics of Neglect: Urban Aid from Model Cities to Revenue Sharing* (Cambridge, Mass.: MIT Press, 1975), 36-98.

15. For examples of such studies, see K. Hanf and F. W. Scharpf (eds.), *Interorganizational Policy Making: Limits to Coordination and Central Control* (Beverly Hills, Calif.: Sage Publications, 1978); W. Williams with B. J. Narver, *Government by Agency* (New York: Academic Press, 1980); and E. R. Alexander, "Sharing Power Among Organizations: Coordination Models to Link Theory and Practice" in *Shared Power* (J. M. Bryson and R. C. Einsweiker, eds.) (Lanham, MD: University Press of America, 1986).

16. E. R. Alexander, "The Limits of Uncertainty: A Note," *Theory and Decision* 6(3) (December 1975): 112-119.

17. These may include individual reactions to collective measures, and other organizations' responses to adopted policies: G. A. Wissink, "The Limits to Planning: A Comment," *Town Planning Review* 51(4) (October 1980): 409-413; see also A. Wildavsky (1979), op. cit., pp. 41-70 for examples of problems which are themselves the product of interventions designed to be solutions.

18. F. H. Tenbruck, *Zur Kritik der Planenden Vernunft* (Freiburg: Verl. K. Alber, 1972), 70.

19. Sir G. Vickers, *Value Systems and Social Process* (New York: Basic Books, 1968), 74.
20. See, for example, the special issue of *The Public Interest* on the Great Society, especially L. Liebman, "Social Intervention in a Democracy," *The Public Interest*, 34 (Winter 1974): 14-29.
21. N. Caiden and A. Wildavsky, *Planning and Budgeting in Poor Countries*, (New York, Wiley, 1974).
22. G. Vickers, *Freedom in a Rocking Boat: Changing Values in an Unstable Society* (London: Allan Lane, 1970).
23, Some examples are: J. Friedmann, *Retracking America: A Theory of Transactive Planning* (New York: Anchor Press/Doubleday, 1973); E. R. Alexander (1973), op. cit., and J. Friedmann (1976), op. cit.
24. M. M. Webber, "Planning in an Environment of Change: Part II—Permissive Planning," *Town Planning Review*, 39(1) (January 1969): 279-280.
25. G. Schubert, *The Public Interest* (Glencoe, Ill.: Free Press, 1960) 223.
26. R. E. Klosterman, "Foundations for Normative Planning," *Journal of the American Institute of Planners*, 44(1) (January 1978): 37-46.
27. R. E. Klosterman, "A Public Interest Criterion," *Journal of the American Planning Association* 46(3) (July 1980): 323-333.
28. J. Friedmann, " The Public Interest and Community Participation: Towards a Reconstruction of Public Philosophy," *Journal of the American Institute of Planners* 39(1) (January 1973): 2, 4-7.
29. J. F. Zimmerman, *The Federated City: Community Control in Large Cities* (New York: St. Martin's Press, 1972), 4.
30. J. H. Strange, "Citizen Participation in Community Action and Model Cities Programs," *Public Administration Review*, 32(3) (October 1965): 655.
31. See S. R. Arnstein, "A Ladder of Citizen Participation," *Journal of the American Institute of Planners* 35(3) (July 1969): 216-224; J. J. Glass, "Citizen Participation in Planning: The Relationship Between Objectives and Techniques," *Journal of the American Planning Association* 45(1) (April 1979): 180-189.
32. M. Fagence, *Citizen Participation in Planning* (Oxford: Pergamon, 1977), 272-330; Glass, op. cit., pp. 182-188; M. G. Kweit and R. W. Kweit, *Implementing Citizen Participation in a Bureaucratic Society* (New York: Praeger, 1981), 34-36, 54-60.
33. See Kweit and Kweit, op. cit., pp. 37-39; Glass, op. cit.
34. Kweit and Kweit, op. cit., pp. 82-103; B. Checkoway and J. Van Til, "What Do We Know About Citizen Participation? A Selective Review of Research," pp. 25-42 in *Citizen Participation in America* (S. Langton, ed.) (Lexington, Mass.: D. C. Heath, 1978), 30-33.
35. M. Fagence, op. cit., pp. 331-355, 370.
36. Checkoway and Van Til, op. cit., pp. 33-34; for some of the organizational characteristics of successful grass-roots groups, see J. E. Perlman, "Grassroots Participation from Neighborhood to Nation," pp. 71-75 in S. Lanton (ed.) op. cit.
37. See Checkoway and Van Til op. cit., p. 37; for a discussion of these questions, see F. F. Piven, *et al.*, "Symposium: Whom Does the Advocate Planner Serve?," *Social Policy*, 1 (May-June 1970): 32-37.

38. American Institute of Planners, *Code of Professional Responsibility*, (Washington, D.C.: American Institute of Planners, 1976), Sec. 1.1 (a).
39. Concerned Architects and Planners, "Ecological Effects of the Vietnam War," *Journal of the American Institute of Planners* 38 (September 1972): 297.
40. P. Marcuse, "Professional Ethics and Beyond: Values in Planning," *Journal of the American Institute of Planners* 42 (July 1976): 272.
41. A. Faludi, *Planning Theory* (Oxford: Pergamon Press, 1973).
42. N. Krumholz, J. M. Cogger, and J. H. Linner, "The Cleveland Policy Planning Report, " *Journal of the American Institute of Planners* 41 (September 1975): 299.
43. An example of such an evaluation addressed to the Cleveland planning experience is: N. Krumholz, J. L. Kaufman, P. Davidoff and L. Susskind, "A Retrospective View of Equity Planning: Cleveland 1969-1979" and "Comment," *Journal of the American Planning Association* 48(2) (Spring 1982): 163-183.
44. Friedmann (1973), op. cit., p. 112.
45. Not only planning, but other respected and sometimes more highly paid professions, such as medicine, law, and education are experiencing the same phenomenon. Witness the proliferation of lay medical review panels, of malpractice suits and the rise in malpractice insurance, the concept of "accountability" in education, and so on.
46. See, for example, A. J. Catanese and P. Farmer (eds.), *Personality, Politics and Planning: How City Planners Work*, (Beverly Hills, Calif.: Sage, 1978).
47. J. L. Kaufman, "Contemporary Planning Practice: State of the Art," pp. 111-137 in *Planning in America: Learning from Turbulence* (D. R. Godschalk, ed.) (Washington, D.C.: AIP, 1974).
48. Based on 1978 random survey of AIP members—see M. L. Vasu, *Politics and Planning: A National Study of American Planners* (Chapel Hill, N.C.: University of North Carolina Press, 1979); and a 1981 survey of 316 city planners and managers—see T. D. Galloway and J. T. Edwards, "Critically Examining the Assumptions of Espoused Theory: The Case of City Planning and Management," *Journal of the American Planning Association* 48(1) (Spring 1982): 184-195.
49. These findings are based on a survey of 616 U.S. planners who are members of the AIP; B. Howe and J. Kaufman, "The Ethics of Contemporary American Planners," *Journal of the American Planning Association* 45(3) (July 1979): 243-255; E. Howe, "Role Choices of Urban Planners," *Journal of the American Planning Association* 46(4) (October 1980): 398-409.
50. The impact of ethics and values on planners' issue-related behavior was tested by simulating real issues in scenarios, and by analyzing actual planning behavior relating to issues such as Environmental Impact Reports and the Pan Am central city redevelopment in New York: P. Marcuse, "Professional Ethics and Beyond: Values in Planning," *Journal of the American Institute of Planners* 42(3) (July 1976): 264-274; Howe and Kaufman, op. cit., pp. 243-251; F. Howe and J. Kaufman, "The Values of Contemporary American Planners," *Journal of the American Planning Association* 47(3) (July 1981): 266-278.
51. R. G. Tugwell, "The Fourth Power," *Planning and Civic Comment*, AIP and Civic Association, April-June 1939; however, though national planning has

never been institutionalized in the United States, it has manifested itself in a variety of forms; see D. E. Wilson, *The National Planning Idea in U.S. Public Policy: Five Alternative Approaches* (Boulder, Colo.: Westview Press, 1980).

52. J. Heller, *As Good as Gold* (New York: Simon and Schuster, 1976, 1979) (Pocket Books, 1980), 73, 76.
53. *The Bhagavad Gita* 3(8) (J. Mascaro, trans.) (Baltimore: Penguin Classics), 56.
54. Some, maintain, in fact, that this has been the case since the development of the modern corporation: J. K. Galbraith, *The New Industrial State* (Boston: Houghton Mifflin, 1967), 22-45; for specifics and examples of strategic planning, see G. Steiner, *Strategic Planning: What Every Manager Must Know*, (New York: Free Press, 1979); P. Lorange, *Implementation of Strategic Planning* (Englewood Cliffs, N.J.: Prentice-Hall, 1982).

INDEX

Financial Institutions, local, participation
in indicative planning 74
Fire resistance codes, example of
regulative planning 72
Firm(s) 7, 67, 72
decisions 74, 98
Fiscal
analyst, as job title of planning-related
position 114
impact 46, 54
management 70
Fish, and EIS 54
Foresight 40, 99
Forester, J. 38, 91
Forests 70
Forethought, as definition of planning 39
Formal organization, and radical/anti-
planning 78
Format 13
Foundations, benevolent, and planners in
entrepreneur role 84
Foundry, steel, smoke emissions from-
example of externalities 96
France 73, 74, 77, 90, 102
French planning: "Le Plan" 74
Frederickson, H. G. 30, 38, 47, 60
Free market(s) 96, 97
Freeways 100, 101
Frieden, B. J. 118
Friedland, E. L. 36
Friedman, M. 35
Friedmann, J. 30, 38, 59, 89, 90, 91,
109, 119, 120
Friedrich, C. J. 118
Friend, J. K. 36, 43, 89, 90, 118
Function(s), planning, delegation of 94
Functional, planning models 66-71
Functions, spatial distribution of, and
physical planning 66
Funding, federal and rise/fall of social
planning agencies 89
Funding agencies, national, and planner in
entrepreneur role 84
Funds
to implement plans and entrepreneur
role 82
budgeting, and allocative planning 72
Future 40, 47, 74, 78, 100, 109, 115
orientation of planning 40, 47
Future action(s), and planning 40, 42
Futures, desirable, and utopian
thinkers 42

Galanter, E. 58
Galbraith, J. K. 121
Galloway, T. D. 9, 37, 120
Game(s), as public participation technique
106
Gans, H. J. 90
Gelberd, L. 37
General Accounting Office, as location of
accepted planning analysis 114
General theory of planning 8
Generic planning 70
Gentrification 101
Geographic levels, of transportation
planning 67
Geology, in environmental planning 70
Germany, West 102
Giannis, N. V. 90
Gibb, J. A. 88
Go-no-Go decision 52
Goal(s) 5, 12, 19, 21, 26, 28, 46-47, 54,
56, 74, 94, 100, 101, 105, 108
and means 26-27
of planning 107-110
of public participation 105-107
planners' 80, 103
social 67, 72
spatial distribution of and physical
planning 66
Goals—Achievement Matrix, and public
interest criterion 104
Goals, Social, and regulatory planning 72
Goldsmith, W. J. 91
Goodman, R. 90
Goods
merit 97
production by governments, public
organizations: public goods 97
pricing of, in oligopolies 96
Government 2, 5-7, 19
and capacity for societal self-
regulation 106
and planners in interpreter/com-
municator roles 84
and planning 42, 71, 72, 76, 93, 99,
102, 104, 114
as producers of public goods 97
city, and advocacy role 82
"good" government and the public
interest 103
in bureaucratic planning 77
muster support, resources in technical/
administrative role 81

Houston TX, & nonplanning 78
Howard, E. 5
Howe, E. 120
Hudson, B. M. 37, 59
Human
  activities: advice & planning as h.a.'s
    83
  behavior 20, 39, 45, 76
  beings, and EIS 54
  growth, and planning goals and values
    108
  nature, and mix between planning/non-
    planning 78
  needs 107-108
  programs, and cost-effectiveness
    analysis 53
  relations, views of, and views of plan-
    ners roles 84
  relationships 99
  services 7, 70, 76
  systems and ecological planning 79
  values, change in, and future need for
    planning 115
Humanness, as planning value 108
Hunch(es) 15
Hurwicz, L. 35
Hybrid, as planners' role 112

IBIS 51
Ideal(s) 51, 87, 112
Ideas, and limits of planning 101
Idealized Design 51
Ideological
  premises, and contextual planning
    models 75
  reorientation, and radical/anti-
    planning 78
  shortcomings of social planning 76
Ideology(ies) 4, 45, 66, 74, 75, 78, 105
Ignorance, and limits of planning 101
Ignorant, resources available to 77
Image
  of planning, and public interest 104
  planners' self 111-113
  planners' self i., and "intractable
    problems" 95
  111, 113
Impact(s) 16, 55, 106
  fiscal 46, 54
  of alternative proposals 48, 52, 104
  of alternatives' evaluation 52
Impact analysis 16, 54

Implementation 13, 19, 41, 48, 52, 55,
  71, 72, 75, 78-79, 81, 94, 99
  tools 50, 67
Implementing agencies 55
Implications
  political, of social planning 76
  of planners role uncertainty 85
Impossibility Theorem 18
Impotence, expert's, and independence
  94
Inaction, as response to perceived importance of planning 113
Incentive(s) 68, 73, 96
Incidence, of costs and benefits, and
  qualitative evaluation approaches 54
Inclusive roles, for planners 83
Income
  from education, as program outcome
    53
  and comprehensive planning 75
Incremental(ism) 21, 23, 30, 47, 80, 118
  decision model 78, 112
  disjointed 42, 109-110
  model 29, 78
Independence, planners', and planners
  expertise 94
Indeterminacy, of ideas, values, meanings,
  and limits of planning 101
Index, journal, and heuristic search 50
Indicative Planning 73-5
Indicator 53
Individual(s) 6, 7, 20, 21, 42
  and public participation 105
  decisions 94, 95, 96, 98
  identification of interests of, and public
    interest 104
  preferences 18
  wants, needs transmitted by market 97
Industrial Location, national policy, and
  regulatory planning 72
Industrial
  design and design of alternatives 49
  investments, and allocation planning 73
  polluters, charged for cleaning costs 96
Industrialization 95
Infallibility, scientific, ambiguity of planners claims to ... 84
Inflation, and limits of planning 100
Influence 19
Information 12-14, 21, 22, 48, 50, 74,
  84, 100, 112
  and public participation 105, 106

140 INDEX

a result of unequal distribution of wealth/income;
the supply of "public" and/or "merit" goods;
and/or "internalizing" the effects of externalities.

ple from your reading and/or experience of each of the
ou have identified as demanding or possibly needing
ention. Describe what form the planning inter ation
en any) has taken in each case.

es not only mean public intervention, identify from
e or experience other forms and arenas of planning.
ing needed in each of the cases you describe?

llowing has/have been invoked as sources for planners'
for others?

expertise and scientific analysis;
nd respond to needs and problems of client

alues;
munities in a joint participatory planning

eaucratic-administrative role;
ernment-elected representative officials;
itical ideology;
th ps being planned with/for.

guments for planners' authority that you have
above do you agree, and which do you re-
your conclusions;

st." Do you agree that such a concept exists?
e, identified and used in planning? If it does
nt tute as a rationale for comprehensive

et of professional ethics—rules to
If so, whe e an they be found?
aims of planning to be a pro-

8. What is the role of "the public interest" in the prof
   planning (if any, and if there are such ethics)? If the
   is included among planners' values, how has this value
   alized? Describe an example and its impacts, if any.

What are some of the roles that professional planne
according to recent research? Which of the followin
the role choices of planners:

(a) Age;
(b) Sex;
(c) Political ideology in general;
(d) The specific issue involved + political orientation
(e) Job context—agency size;
(f) Job context—geographic location of state;
(g) Job context—large or small city.

10. What do you see as the future of planning? Descri
    that planning might perform in the society of the fu
    some emerging sectors that will call for planning and
    In which other sectors may planning become routi
    formed into bureaucratic-administrative activities? I
    self being involved in any of the pl   ing-related re
    scribed? If you do, give some of your reasons, and
    would see yourself carrying out your planning activitie

Notes

1. John W. Dyckman, "The Practical Uses of Planning Theor
    American Institute of Planners, (September 1969): 299.
2. See, for example, A. Altshuler, op. cit., A. J. Catanese, op c
    and R. L. Nuttall, Urban Planning and Politics (Lexington, :
    1975); an insightful discussion of the role of planning expe
    site, op. cit.; see especially D. Eversley, The Planner in Soci
    Role of a Profession (Faber and Faber, 1973).
    Martin Rein, "Social Planning: The Search for Legitimac"
    merican Institute of Planne   July 1969): 24 3.
    Garrett Hardin, " The Tragedy of the Commons," Scienc
    1968: 1243-1248.
    An   to   body of literature in welfare economics deal
    for a valu.   p.   g b   se
    T. Moore, op cr.